Stephan

**Celebrating Haywards Heath:
Heart of Sussex**

John Twisleton

David,
thank you for your support in all mayoral stuff and Merry Christmas, Stephane

John Twisleton

With South Downs & London rail trails

Commendations for
Celebrating Haywards Heath: Heart of Sussex

This book draws together other writings about Haywards Heath in the author's own very readable style. It gives a fascinating insight into the development of an area of heathland originally known as "Hayworth" which has grown into such a thriving town with, among others, religious communities, tourists visiting the South Downs and commuters. A very worthwhile read on the train to London.

Sir James Dingemans

As a relative newcomer to Haywards Heath it is wonderful to have such a compressive history of the town development. 'Celebrating Haywards Heath: Heart of Sussex' is a work that delves into the rich tapestry of this charming town's past. The book brings to life the significant events, personalities, and cultural shifts that have shaped Haywards Heath over the years and paints a compelling picture of the town's evolution, from its early days to its current status as a vibrant community. This book is both informative and visually captivating. It is an indispensable resource for local historians, residents, and anyone with an interest in the heritage of Haywards Heath. The author's ability to combine scholarly research with engaging prose makes this book a delightful read, ensuring that the history of Haywards Heath will be appreciated by generations to come.

Canon David King
Parish Priest of St Richard, Haywards Heath

I have had the privilege of growing up in Sussex and know that many move to Haywards Heath in particular because it is such an ideal place to live, work and raise a family. Its connectivity to the city and the coast has always attracted people in a pragmatic way, but those that choose to settle here recognise that the town has much more to offer than a quick train. Spend some time in our town and you too will realise we have some of the most fantastic businesses, vibrant community groups and precious green spaces. But as our town continues to grow and we welcome new residents to the heart of Sussex, the story of Haywards Heath should be more readily available. Regrettably, (at the time of writing) there is little local history that can be easily accessed by the public and there is no Haywards Heath Museum. I feel that the preservation and sharing of local history is critical to establishing the identity and culture of the town, especially for the new residents we welcome here. Thankfully, there are passionate members of our community in Haywards Heath that want to preserve its history and share its stories, for this, I am grateful to John Twisleton for persevering with this book. It is through the efforts of people like John that a community arts and culture board has now been formed at the town council to help coordinate cultural activities. With a community-led approach, I wish for this book to form part of a staging ground for a Haywards Heath museum, where the Town's history can be told in ways that are illustrative and engaging; its success will be owed to the hard work of local historians like John.

Councillor Duncan Pascoe
Deputy Mayor - Haywards Heath Town Council

Having lived in Haywards Heath for all of my 74 years, and loving the history of our town, this book provides a very accurate picture of the town in days gone by. As a relative newcomer to the town, John quite obviously demonstrates that he shares my passion with the history of Haywards Heath, and by involving local primary school pupils, hopefully some of those children will equally share that passion as they become the adults of the future. With the population of our town having increased from under 10,000 in the 1950s, to currently in excess of 40,000, the suggestion of a local museum should also be applauded, as it will hopefully contribute to the town's ongoing history, for the benefit of many future generations, and newcomers to our town. I found this book to be an easy and enjoyable read, and feel certain it will be enjoyed by very many.

Charles Tucker
Creator of Facebook Group 'Haywards Heath in days gone by'

Copyright © 2024 JohnTwisleton

All rights reserved.
ISBN: 979-8322378303

Acknowledgments

The author acknowledges the substantive inspiration to his work of Wyn Ford and Conway Gabe, 'The Metropolis of Mid-Sussex - A History of Haywards Heath' (1981), Margaret Nicolle, 'William Allen, Quaker Friend of Lindfield' (2001) and conversations with the late Fr Ray Smith, former Rector of St Wilfrid's. Quotations from these sources and others John would also acknowledge are linked through numbers in the text to page references listed in the Notes at the end of the book.

Since 2018 John Twisleton has published blog posts on Instagram, Twitter and Haywards Heath Community, Haywards Heath in days gone by and Bentswood Community Partnership Facebook Groups. The author acknowledges those involved with him in online discussion there, especially Charles Tucker, in refining his knowledge of the town's history. Fr John acknowledges the inspiration of staff and pupils at St Wilfrid's Church of England School whose summer term 2024 history project is celebrated as a Postscript. John Twisleton is grateful to Haywards Heath Town Council for their encouragement to raise the profile of town history through this book.

The author further acknowledges permission to reproduce photographs from the collections of Cuckfield Museum, Charles Tucker and David Tucker. Fr John presents apologies in advance for any omission in acknowledgement. As the book hopefully evidences, his aim in writing is to celebrate and build on previous writings drawing out the main lines of the history of Haywards Heath from those more informed than himself.

Foreword by the Mayor of Haywards Heath

I have been living in Haywards Heath for over 11 years now. We moved back to the UK after a few years abroad, and like for quite a few people, Haywards Heath was a strategic location. Indeed, for its proximity to London enhanced by the frequent commuter trains from the station, its proximity to Gatwick Airport threshold to the world, and of course also its proximity to Brighton and the seaside with the occasional seagulls to remind us of it. Once I moved to Haywards Heath, something became clear very quickly: Haywards Heath had much more to offer than "accessibility to somewhere else"! Haywards Heath is indeed a beautiful and vibrant place in its own right, a local centre in its own right even. We are surrounded by idyllic countryside which I enjoy everyday as my house looks onto the South Downs. Nature is present everywhere, whether it is in the impeccably manicured Muster Green, to beautiful Victoria Park, to the wonderful gardens, some private, some communal, which are spread all over our town. We are a proud burst of nature within the Green Belt and a much awarded one, including Green Flag Awards, Haywards Heath In Bloom, and even entering Britain in Bloom!

Our community never ceases to amaze me! As Mayor, I am the champion of our community and that includes supporting and promoting our local businesses and charities. Our community spirit is second to none and it shines through the selflessness of the many of residents who volunteer their time, the generosity of the local businesses who sponsor community events, the environmental push and momentum being achieved by service, manufacturing, and high tech businesses based right here within our town.

And we are a talented lot! Performing Arts schools have been blooming in recent years, and so have concerts by local artists, exhibitions, the nostalgic and beautiful restored Bluebell Railway Steam Trains, our very own Haywards Heath Town Football Team women, men and youngsters, and more! The schools are always keen to give their pupils a chance to develop their creativity, like the Butterfly Artworks that were produced for Holocaust Day 2023. We now have plenty of yearly events that proudly display our fun and artistic side: Rotary Rocks, Haywards Heath Got Talent, and of course the amazing Hayward Heath Art Festival every year, and that is just to name a few!

We are a caring community as we tirelessly and joyfully care for each other and for our town, our home. John Twisleton's book gives fascinating insight and background into our Haywards Heath and how it developed into the town as we know it today. It is not only a precious historical document and legacy, but I have to tell you that you will find that it reads like a beautiful love letter...

Councillor Stephanie Inglesfield   July 2024

Contents

Title page		
Commendations		1
Copyright		4
Acknowledgments		5
Foreword		6
1	Heart of Sussex	10
	Introduction	
2	Commanding heights	16
	The High Weald	
3	London's love for Brighton	22
	The Railway	
4	The Dolphin	28
	Cuckfield origins	
5	William Allen	34
	Lindfield origins	
6	The Cattle Market	40
	Farming past and present	
7	Place of therapy	46
	The Asylum and hospitals	
8	Enterprising hub	52
	Commuter town	
9	Schooling and recreation	58
	Education, sports and leisure	
10	Spiritual mecca	64
	Religion and tourism	
Postscript - St Wilfrid's School project		70
Timeline		76
Index		80
Notes		84

Appendix 1 - South Downs walks via Haywards Heath station
                                                        86
Appendix 2 - London sights via Haywards Heath station   94
Appendix 3 - History of Presentation Church   100
About the author   106
Haywards Heath - a poem by the author   110

1   **Heart of Sussex**
Introduction

Anne and I have lived in Haywards Heath or its surrounds since 2001. My posting in Chichester Diocese brought us to the town so I could travel all over Sussex at minimum cost in the service of parish revitalisation. It made sense to live in a Church house in Gatesmead right at the heart of Sussex from where I travelled east to Rye, west to Chichester, north to Crawley and south to Brighton. I moved to be Rector of Horsted Keynes in 2009, a village that looks to the town, and retired to Marylands off New England Road in 2017. This is now my base for ongoing involvement in the town community as writer, priest, blogger and broadcaster (1). I have spent a third of my life at the heart of Sussex in a community of gifted people many of whom seek to use their gifts in service of fellow residents. My own gifts are used in helping provide digital access, promoting walking, spiritual direction, helping churches and exploring local history. During 2024 I have been helping pupils at St Wilfrid's School engage with older inhabitants to draw out their wisdom including stories of Haywards Heath 'in days gone by'. My friend Charles Tucker, former local policeman, runs a Facebook Group of that name with 8,400 members, a fifth of the town's population of 40,184 (2021 census) which indicates widespread interest in the town's history (2). The group and my own blogging have prompted me to write this broad-brush stroke town history book to kindle further interest and commitment such as finding hosting and volunteers to service a Haywards Heath Museum. It is a celebration of the town framed by myself, drawing on authoritative sources and linked to my walk books. I beg the forbearance of readers in this construction.

Haywards Heath is viewed as a commuter town that grew up after the arrival of the railway in 1841 though it is much more than that. From a tourism vantage point there is a 'going out from here' parallel to commuting. My book has the secondary aim, linked to my 'Fifty Walks from Haywards Heath' (2020), of indicating best routes to sights in Sussex and London from Haywards Heath station (3). Just as tourists use our town as base, the majority of residents find employment away from the town in Brighton & Hove, Crawley, Gatwick Airport and London. My primary aim in writing is to remind readers that Haywards Heath is a place to be celebrated for its own sake and, whilst a commuter town, should also draw interest on account of its own history. This stretches back not just to 1841 but to the establishing of the 'Hayworth' enclosure first mentioned 1265-6 through Philip and then Thomas both 'of Hayworth'.

The title 'Celebrating Haywards Heath: Heart of Sussex' was chosen to resonate with the title of the substantive town history by Wyn Ford and Conway Gabe 'The Metropolis of Mid Sussex - A History of Haywards Heath' (1981). That book's introduction makes it clear: 'Haywards Heath 'must be the Metropolis of Mid-Sussex'. That was the opinion expressed by representatives of St Wilfrid's Church in December 1877. In support of this they made a number of observations. The population was increasing, and the town now catered for the majority of the town of Cuckfield. The Primitive Methodists had recently opened a chapel in South Road, and the Congregationalist had already been established in Wivelsfield Road further down in 1861; in both, the staff of the Sussex County Lunatic Asylum had active members. Furthermore, the railway station saw upwards of seventy train each day' (4).

My book celebrates the remote origin of Haywards Heath in an ancient crossroads on the commanding heights of the High Weald. Roman roads from the coast to London crossed these heights descending through Cuckfield and Lindfield. Two thousand years on London's love affair with Brighton and the south coast fuelled demand for the railway. Cuckfield and Lindfield caused and shaped the growth of Haywards Heath. Both well established communities shunned the new metal road steering it in between the villages on a track parallel to the ancient road to London creating a station on the 'Hayworth' which became the hub and heart of Sussex. Cuckfield shaped the new town by building a daughter Church, St Wilfrid's, to Holy Trinity and by the patronage of landowners including the Burrell's and Sergison's. This book chronicles how Lindfield made its mark on the heath just before the railway's arrival through the munificence of William Allen (1770-1843). Seeing the large number of poor people in Lindfield, Allen devised a scheme in which families were given land to build their own cottages and to farm part of the south of the heath now Bentswood's America estate. 'Celebrating Haywards Heath' tells of his philanthropy and that of others such as the Rotary Club in helping create Franklands Village a century later. The book's narrative relates how the arrival of the railway came to serve farming across Sussex through the weekly cattle market. This celebration of Haywards Heath continues recording the choice of the town for the Sussex County Asylum and how innovative practice there paved the way for therapeutic engagement with mental illness. Later chapters look at commerce, education, sports and leisure concluding with religion and tourism. In the 19th and early 20th century Haywards Heath became something of a spiritual mecca with a burgeoning number of churches, convents and retreat houses. The great Gothic Priory Chapel and Convent built 1891 housed a community of sisters for almost a century. The Convent's long high walls gave the town something of a forbidding feel until they were taken down to facilitate the current residential estate after the sisters left. The Chapel remains as the largest monument in town and is now itself reordered for housing. The spiritual focus of Haywards Heath Churches were and are, along with other secular and religious bodies including today the Islamic Centre, inseparable from service of the needy. Ford and Gabe record: 'In the hard times of 1894, St Wilfrid's Church was actively concerned with a soup kitchen. It opened on the first Saturday in January for about 10 weeks, during which time around 800 quarts of soup were sold at a penny a quart and over 600 loaves of bread were sold at the same price a loaf' (5). In 2024 St Wilfrid's daughter Church of the Presentation provides a free soup lunch once a week which is well received in Bentswood. Though Haywards Heath has affluence, as in 1894 it is alongside pockets of poverty with the current hike in the cost of living making spiritual outreach in the form of soup kitchens just as relevant. 'Celebrating Haywards Heath: Heart of Sussex' ends with another spiritual outreach, that of tourism using the town as a base through Appendices with best routes to sights in Sussex and London from Haywards Heath station supplementing my provision in 'Fifty Walks from Haywards Heath'.

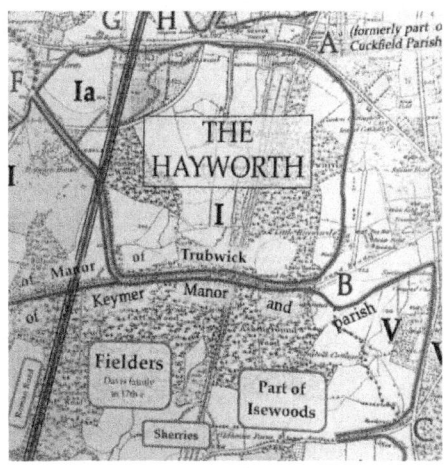

Historical map in Cuckfield Museum mentioning Hayworth

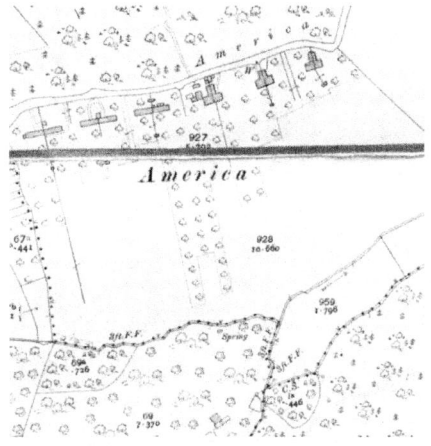

Cuckfield Museum map of America colony

JOHN TWISLETON

2 Commanding heights
The High Weald

With the extensive building in Haywards Heath we are less aware of our original situation on an age-old trail along the heights of Mid Sussex at one time thought to be part of the pilgrim route from Winchester to Canterbury. This idea certainly influenced the people of Scaynes Hill on A272 who dedicated their Church to St Augustine of Canterbury in this spirit. The main east-west pilgrim routes of the Middle Ages are now considered to have been along the better drained North and South Downs.

The east-west ridge the town of Haywards Heath is built upon runs across Mid Sussex parallel to the M25 and A27 traversing the north and the south. The latest large housing project in the town has been the creation in 2002 of Bolnore Garden Village. This was an attempt to recover our forested origin which had an agreement built in to create Haywards Heath by-pass that opened in 2014. Consequently the A272 traversing the commanding heights of Mid Sussex was diverted around town where its original route is now renamed B2272.

As a resident of Haywards Heath and its surrounds over 23 years the most difficult years for me and for many were 2020-21 when the COVID pandemic restricted movement. Over that period I extended my walking and discovered a treasury of routes south of the town which became the origin of my 'Fifty Walks from Haywards Heath'. This latest book with its rail trails is something of a supplement and is also the fruit of my keener engagement with fellow local historians and bloggers. Slowing down, appreciating a gentler pace of life and discovering more of what's on the doorstep brought new inspiration. In particular the slowing of traffic in the air and on the roads facilitated discovery. For many residents the busy A272 Lewes Road is a daunting barrier but that became less so as traffic reduced in Lockdown. It was easier to reflect upon the strategic significance of that road and the town's origins on an ancient crossroads on this high ridge looking both south to Brighton, South Downs and the sea and north to London whose southern boundary rests along the North Downs. During Lockdown it was easier to discover the roads and footpaths south from Lewes Road. Slugwash Lane - a delightful title linked to low land or slough rather than slugs - became a portal to delights such as the Cottage of Content, Abbots Leigh House and Wivelsfield. 'As the M25 skirts the North Downs south of London and the A27 skirts the South Downs and Brighton the A272 traverses the ancient home of Haywards Heath, the High Weald of Mid-Sussex. Heather Warnes 2009 history observes that 'it was common in this part of Mid Sussex for early estates to be laid out across a ridge top, the north-facing slopes often being reserved to the lord for wood and timber'. The heath was open land facing south benefitting both from the sun and drainage of water from the rock underlay of the High Weald down to the southern claylands. Wivelsfield Green east of the historic village of Wivelsfield is part of the Low Weald [accessed as you descend Slugwash Lane] towards the South Downs visible on the horizon' (6).

Parallel to celebrating Haywards Heath this book celebrates the access the town provides to beauty spots along the South Downs Way and within The High Weald Area of Outstanding Natural

Beauty so assigned in 1982. This covers an area of 1,450 square kilometres taking up parts of Kent, Surrey, East Sussex, and West Sussex. It is the fourth largest Area of Outstanding Natural Beauty in England and Wales. Writing of the Weald a few years before that assignment Ford & Gabe inform us: 'The area in Kent and Sussex known as the Weald derives its name from the great wood that extended between the North and South Downs from the Kent coast around Folkestone as far as Petersfield in Hampshire. Fifteen hundred years ago, we are told, Aelle and his companions drove the Britons into 'the wood which is called *Andredsleah*' after they had landed at Selsey. The hint that they were deterred by the density of the trees is supported by other evidence. When William the Conqueror came to found his Abbey at Battle, the site was chosen for its remoteness, and the principal remains of earlier periods are clustered on the Downs. Yet it would be quite wrong to regard the Weald as an impenetrable jungle uninhabited before modern times. There was an iron industry from Roman times, with workings in the West Hoathly/East Grinstead area' (7) Where there is wood there is fuel, scope for trade and building settlements. Passage along the heights of the A272 three centuries back would have seemed less tranquil. There would have been the incessant hammering of iron echoing everywhere from the Weald's hammer ponds. At that time the draw of the sea, though important for defence and trade, was less. Only in the late eighteenth century did turnpike roads open Sussex up and counter an inward-looking tendency. The county anthem 'Sussex by the Sea' was written by William Ward-Higgs as late as 1907. By then the railway had arrived facilitating mass access to the south coast via Haywards Heath.

'In 1965, in his introduction to the original *Buildings of England*, Ian Nairn saw the difference between Surrey ('most of which is fatally turned towards London') and Sussex as 'huge'. Since then, however, improvements to the roads from London to the coast in the eastern half of West Sussex (the M23 was created south of the M25 in 1972-5) and closure in 1966 of much of the network of branch railways have reinforced the links to the capital and the feeling in much of the county of subjugation to it; the houses of well-healed commuters can be glimpsed through foliage on leafy lanes or clustering round popular villages and towns. The east-west connections, except along the coast via the A27 and the South Coast railway, are much poorer, so that there are still miles and miles of preserved countryside bolstered by a multitude of healthy bank balances, especially as one goes west' (8)

The east-west ridge Haywards Heath stands upon is a popular route for sightseeing motorists. The A272 in Sussex is always less than 40 miles from London. It commands scenic views of age old countryside and, save in its circuit of Haywards Heath, escapes any heavily built up areas whilst passing through some of the most charming villages in the UK.

Fred Miller's commanding painting St Wilfrid's in winter 1880 uses artistic licence to emphasise its prominence.

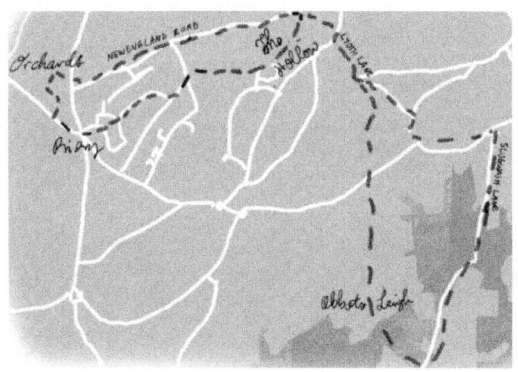

Walk 25 from 'Fifty Walks from Haywards Heath' drawn by Rebecca Twisleton descends the Weald via Slugwash Lane

JOHN TWISLETON

3 London's love for Brighton
The Railway

London's love affair with Brighton traces back to the championing of sea bathing and sea air as healing remedies in the eighteenth century. Fuelled by royalty interest in Brighton grew so that the flow of up to 40 coaches a day left the capital leading to the arrival of the railway in 1841. An Act of Parliament in July 1837 had previously given the green light for the building of the London and Brighton Railway. Before this date the landowners of Cuckfield on the old London and Brighton Road had successfully resisted the construction of the railway through their village by buying up all of the land. Building the railway through Cuckfield would have given a more direct and unobstructed route from the Balcombe Tunnel to the Clayton Tunnel. As a result of this resistance, the construction of the railway was made more difficult and the London to Brighton railway was instead routed across the heath – the rail track being laid in a cutting and a tunnel through the highest point of the heath. The wooded spoil heap is there today alongside Victoria Park, a remarkable feat of construction, which employed many railway labourers, or navvies, with more than a hundred being recorded as resident locally in the 1841 Census. The earthworkings and the tunnel across Haywards Heath were not the only remarkable pieces of local railway infrastructure caused by this diversion. Just one-mile north of Haywards Heath is the Balcombe Viaduct - 96 feet high at its highest point, and 1,475 feet long, designed by John Rastrick. It crosses the Ouse Valley with its thirty seven brick arches. Some twelve and a half million bricks were brought up the river by barge for the construction of this viaduct between 1839 and

1841, half of those being laid under the ground as foundations. The rail track for the London and Brighton Railway was opened between London Bridge and Haywards Heath Station on 12th July 1841 with a temporary halt in place just before the tunnel entrance in the cutting, ahead of the station. At first four trains a day ran to London Bridge on weekdays in each direction and three on Sundays and for just over two months passengers were carried between Haywards Heath and Brighton by horse-coach. The commercial building in Haywards Heath thereafter spread from the Cattle Market and the Station Approach and along Boltro Road on the side of the road backing onto the railway cutting. With the opening of the whole 50-mile route between London Bridge and Brighton (using the London & Croydon Railway line to London Bridge) on 21st September 1841, the new railway soon encouraged the growth of the town of Haywards Heath, and the associated decline of the coaching services and coaching inns upon which Cuckfield's prosperity had previously been founded. Haywards Heath became an important railway hub for the division and connection of trains from along the south coast railway, a system of train movements which remains in place today (9).

Building a railway and a town was thirsty work. A number of pubs and hotels came in their wake starting with the Liverpool Arms for workers on one side of the railway facing the Station Inn across the rails used by employers. Most colourful of all pubs in Haywards Heath's living memory, the Liverpool was built 1851 on the site of the 'Hit or Miss' beer shop frequented by railway labourers. Its dedication recalls workers' Irish origin. Liverpool's original clientele contrasted with that of the Station Inn across the railway frequented by the new town's elite, a fine building still visible from Platform 4. 1960s landlord and former lorry driver Jimmy Munt's 'ain't you got no homes to go to' call at closing time lives in the memory of couples who courted there. Haywards Heath College brought some illegal trade in later years but Liverpool's closure and demolition around 1990 was widely lamented.

In their authoritative town history Ford & Gabe reflect on how 170 years ago 'the increasing prosperity of the 'Liverpool Arms' probably owed something to the policy of railway companies at 'refreshment stations' in providing facilities on either side of the line, although as we have suggested, its clientele was markedly different from that of the Station Inn, and the Inn seems always to have been a private concern. The 'Arms' at one time catered for engine drivers on the down line, but in 1856 the Inn attracted attention of a different kind, when a handbook for railway travellers noted that 'there is a tolerable inn close to the Haywards Heath station, where carriages may be hired'. A later writer grudgingly admitted that it might have been a good inn, for aught I know, in ordinary times', but grumbled that 'the best rooms were all engaged' by one of 'these visitors from London, with their 'piles of money, and unlimited orders for all the best rooms' (10).

Haywards Heath continues to both share and benefit from Londoners' love for Brighton and the South Coast. In 2014 the station was redeveloped to make it a more accessible hub with extensive car parking suited also to those visiting the newly built Premier Inn, sign of the town's developing tourism. Living in Haywards Heath for 23 years and linked for most of that time to St Richard's Church by the station, a 21 min ride from

Brighton Station, has served my exploration of that city and the South Downs. In 2022 I published 'Thirty Walks from Brighton Station' (11). My motivation for writing was linked, as a historian, to love for Brighton & Hove and Haywards Heath, as a walker, to the replenishment of body, mind and spirit attained in that pursuit and as an environmentalist to the provision of handbooks for recreation with low carbon footprint. Two hundred and sixty six sights are listed in the new book, with commentary on a good few of them, constituting an unique exploration of the city and its surrounds, reaching beyond the daytripper's duo of Pier and Pavilion. How many of us have visited Brighton castle - the hill fort up at Hollingbury? Or seen the stone circus pony in Brighton Cemetery? The Sassoon Mausoleum, now a Kemp Town club? Chattri Memorial up the Downs? Or climbed Truleigh Hill to look at the windmills out to sea knowing the power from them is travelling right under you to Twineham substation just up the road from Haywards Heath?

The flow of power to Mid Sussex from windmills off Brighton & Hove is a reminder of how London's love affair with Brighton which triggered our railway and the growth of Haywards Heath is being reciprocated.

With railroad plans for Haywards Heath came concern for stagecoach horses put out to grass as in this Victorian cartoon displayed in Cuckfield Museum.

The Liverpool Hotel around 1990

JOHN TWISLETON

4 The Dolphin
Cuckfield origins

The Station Inn and Liverpool Arms trace back to the railway's arrival in 1841. Before them there was The Dolphin situated on the ancient crossroads which the railway would make the heart of Sussex. This building, now Miller & Carter Steakhouse, is marked as Hen Davis House on the 1638 Map. In 1832 this became the town's first pub, 'The Dolphin', later 'Sergison Arms', named after Charles Sergison who bought Cuckfield Park in 1691 after a naval career. The three dolphins on the family coat of arms give rise to Haywards Heath's 'Dolphin' associations which include the name of the town's Leisure Centre. They provide the town with a cheerful collaborative symbol and reminder of our Cuckfield origins. Ford & Gabe provide a helpful superimposition of the 1638 Map on the 1978 Ordnance Survey Map denoting where nineteen original buildings like 'Pennies' (1606) part of Dinnage's garage on Franklynn Road and The Dolphin pub situated off the ancient Muster Green still exist. West of the Green beyond the pub along Butler's Green Road lie Steeple Cottage, the old Court House, and Butler's Green House linked to Cuckfield's Warden/Sergison family, both houses shown on the 1638 map, as is the map's commissioner Nicholas Hardham's Manor House, Great Haywards Farm (c1400) south of Muster Green down Amberley Close off Bolnore Road. Muster Green is clearly one of the oldest historical sites in Haywards Heath being the northern boundary of the ancient 'Hayworth' enclosure on the 1638 map. The new town sprang up east of Muster Green after the arrival of the railway in 1841. Today it is the site of the town's war memorial dedicated in 1924. What was mustered?

Animals according to a 13th century charter but the battle of Haywards Heath in 1642 gathered troops here or near here as the Council authorised sign explains: 'Here was the site of the Battle of Haywards Heath in December 1642, when a parliamentarian force defeated an invading royalist army and so retained the south-east of England in the hands of Parliament, which ultimately prevailed. So were the seeds of parliamentary government sown. The war started in August 1642 when increasing tension between King Charles I and Parliament, and hostility to the King in London, caused him to withdraw to Nottingham. Soon after this his court moved to Oxford, and most of the north, midlands, Wales and the south west rallied to him. Apart from a few enclaves, Parliament held eastern England, London and the south-east, so a royalist attack on London in November 1642, ending in the indecisive Battle of Turnham Green, was a perilous moment. But a second royalist army invaded the south-east at the start of December 1642, under Sir Edward Ford, the High Sheriff of Sussex. This force moved from Hampshire into Sussex, threatening both the key iron industry and London. After camping at Cuckfield overnight it was met and defeated by a Parliamentarian army under Sir William Waller here at Muster Green, which was then open heathland. Parliament received news of the victory on 8th December 1642. The threat to Parliament was therefore removed, and it was able to turn the tide and ultimately achieve victory in 1646. The restoration of King Charles II in 1660 was on the condition of sharing power with Parliament, from which our democracy eventually grew' (12). Another civic memorial which is more questionable hangs above the pavement in Heath Road. Nasty experiences with highwaymen on the heath east of Cuckfield are part of folklore to the extent of the seeming invention of a fearsome Jack Hayward who once ruled it to whom you had to 'stand and deliver'! This legend colours the town's origins due to ignorance of the town's title deriving from the 'Hayworth' enclosure first mentioned 1265-6. Cuckfield's formative influence upon the new town of Haywards Heath is evident from arrival in the town. At the station visitors are greeted by The Burrell Arms (1871) named to recall the land owning family based at Cuckfield's Ockenden Manor. The Arms on the pub wall with a triumphant arm waving a laurel branch are a copy of Gerald Burrell's (d1599) in Cuckfield Church. Walking under the railway bridge from the Burrell Arms visitors soon reach The Dolphin Leisure Centre (1976) named by association with the Warden Sergison family as are some schools. Settling dispersal of the Sergison estate Haywards Heath was a protracted business leading to a private Act of Parliament in 1853. 'Thereafter matters progressed. The enclosure Act of 1858, and the details were settled by an award at the beginning of 1862. The schedule to the award demonstrates widespread interest. Both local people and more distant men are included. As well as Thomas William Best, a Cuckfield brewer, James Ellis, a Lindfield innkeeper, Charles Knight, the Cuckfield ironmonger, Daniel Knight, also a Cuckfield tradesman, and the Reverend R.E. Wyatt, who was to be the first vicar of St Wilfrid's... in the earliest stages of the town growth, however, two names are especially prominent. The first of these is Richard Pannett... aged 43, with a prosperous business as a carpenter employing six men and a boy... and Thomas Bannister...a Cuckfield man aged 29... who started the cattle market in the mid-1860s, and by 1879 he was advertising himself as 'auctioneer, valued and estate agent, Haywards Heath' (13). 'In January 1856 Cuckfield Curate, The

Revd James Cooper held the first Anglican Service on Sunday afternoons in the loft above a carpenter's shop where Great Heathmead now stands. The Revd Robert Wyatt continued the loft services until the building of the Church School opposite the Star Hotel in Haywards Heath. The School site, then at the very edge of the town, was given by Mr Warden Sergison of Cuckfield Park, the Lord of the Manor of Cuckfield. From 16th December 1856 Matins and Evensong were held in the School Building every Sunday and Holy Communion held once every fortnight. The population of Haywards Heath at this time was around 400. At first known as the Chapel School, the school was opened on 1st April 1857, with Mr Newington as the first Headmaster. The Church Services continued on each Sunday in the School with the sanctuary area shut off "...all the week by folding doors". The School Chapel held 200 people and was by 1863 unable to accommodate those who wished to come, especially in summer time when "...very many were turned away." (Letter by R.E. Wyatt 1863). Usually those who were 'turned away' were from the working classes and the poor, as they wished to avoid a scramble for seats with the upper and middle classes. On 9th January 1862 the site near to the very highest point in Haywards Heath was provided by Mr Sergison for the building of a church' (14) Cuckfield Curate Robert Wyatt had seen George Bodley restore Holy Trinity, Cuckfield and commissioned him to design St Wilfrid's 1863-5 to serve the community created by the railway's arrival. Bodley's creation towers over Haywards Heath, striking in its noble simplicity. The Gothic revival style affirms continuity through the Reformation of the Church of England, 'the ancient church of this land, catholic and reformed' (Revised Catechism). The stained glass windows in the tower by William Morris were gifted by two sisters in memory of their brother, scholar priest John Mason Neale who founded one of the first post-Reformation orders of nuns in East Grinstead. Priests from Cuckfield led services in Haywards Heath until St Wilfrid's became a separate parish in 1910.

Sergison coat of arms

Country pursuits early 20th century outside the Dolphin Pub aka Sergison Arms now Miller & Carter Steakhouse

JOHN TWISLETON

5 William Allen
Lindfield origins

The populating of Haywards Heath began ten years before the railway's arrival in 1841 through an initiative for social renewal led by William Allen. Allen (1770-1843) was raised a Quaker with a burning passion for justice. As a teenager, he gave up sugar in reaction to the slave trade and later worked with William Wilberforce and others to abolish the trade. To quote Allen, 'in the multitude of things which harness the mind, the main object is the good of others'. It was such humanitarian concern to improve the plight of agricultural workers that first brought him to Lindfield. Sussex author Charles Fleet described Lindfield in 1824 as 'eaten up with pauperism'. So many soldiers released after the Napoleonic Wars added to the numbers dependent on poor relief. Into this scenario Allen, supported by the Earl of Chichester and John Smith MP, acquired land to build the school that is now Pelham Cottages. The aim was to educate the children of agricultural labourers furthering their industry and independence. Allen writes of his personal involvement through regular visits: 'I had three of the boys to tea this evening... showed them Saturn, the Moon, etc through the large telescope' (15). The young people gained from the knowledge and care of this enthusiastic scientist and philanthropist. Beyond such mentoring Allen was concerned to improve the nutrition, diet and self-sufficiency of the Lindfield poor. In the early 19th century bad harvests made life tough for small holders. Allen developed a scheme for reducing poor relief in Lindfield involving providing housing, land, cows and pigs for labourers to build self sufficiency through moving their families the short distance to what is now Bentswood into an agricultural colony, 'America' near Bents Wood. The philanthropist's knowledge of nutrition helped him plan allotments to build self-sufficiency and empower agricultural workers from Lindfield. It was a grand social experiment: building a self-sufficient agricultural settlement. In his pamphlet 'Colonies at Home' Allen states 'instead of encouraging emigration at enormous expense per head let the money be applied to the establishment of Colonies at Home and the increase of our national strength' (16). In the 1820s colonies evoked America and that became the name of the project which has left its mark on Haywards Heath with an America Estate with street names chosen to honour Allen's benevolent venture as part of housing built later that century as the new town was built up. One of the most famous inhabitants of Gravelye Lane - William Allen's house still stands with its bell in the roof tower used to summon the community - our local benefactor was a man of many parts. Prior to setting up the nearby allotments Allen helped set up in 1815 a society to investigate the causes of juvenile delinquency. In Margaret Nicolle's 'William Allen' we read his journal record: 'Had a large meeting on the subject of the gangs of depredators from 9 to 12 years of age who infest the metropolis; they are estimated at from 600 to 700. Some of them have been capitally convicted at the Old Bailey, and received sentence of death' (17). In this passage from the same source we read Allen's contemporary Christine Majolier's description of life at Gravelye, the cottage which Allen occupied when he stayed in Lindfield. His house was, she states, ever open to receive 'all strangers who required his aid and protection. Men of all countries, Russians, Germans, Frenchmen, Swedes, Greeks, Italians, Spaniards, North American Indians, West Indians and many of the suffering sons of West Africa partaking of that hospitality, which he knew so well how to bestow without the least ostentation... many a stranger in a strange land has indeed found in him a true friend' (18).

The Brighton Herald (1852) describes a visit to Gravelye cottages in Haywards Heath's America estate: 'The mistress of the house - a good-looking woman - was busily engaged in drying her clothes surrounded by half a dozen children, who had just come from school; the woman was cheerful; the children happy; and there was that unmistakable air of comfort which bespeaks abundance. The wife opened the doors of the sleeping-rooms and the bed-hanging and bed-clothes were as white as snow. The husband showed me his woodhouse and piggery and garden - the latter full of fine fruit trees, planted chiefly by himself' (19).

How successful was Allen's historic allotment scheme at Bentswood? In her biography Margaret Nicolle quotes the philanthropist writing in 1830: 'My object in taking Gravelye Farm was to prove, by an experiment under the public eye, that it is possible to render the agricultural labourer independent of parish relief, even with his present very low wages, by letting him have a little land upon fair terms and directing him in the cultivation of it' (20). Some said lack of manure due to lack of cows and horses made for difficulty. Others judged the experiment a success socially and morally but not financially.

Allen's self-sufficient colony built as Gravelye Cottages known as 'Little America' was situated more or less where the America Lane Parade of shops are now. They lay between the mini roundabouts at the bottom of New England Road and at the junction with Barn Cottage Lane. These cottages remained until just before the second world war, and in due course the area now known as Bentswood was created out of the woods owned by Mr Bent, and the more modern houses and shops in America Lane were built. Many of the roads we know today owe their names to the Council's deliberate association of the new estate with the former Little America Colony, e.g. America Lane, Boston Road, New England Road, Mayflower Road, Quaker Lane, Allen Road and several others. The local pub, now a convenience store, was called at various times the Pilgrim, the Golden Eagle and the Mayflower with the same association. 'Approximately 1938 they demolished the last cottage in Little America. At this time Hiltons the builders were building the houses in Allen road. Number one and number three have stone work from these cottages incorporated in the external walls. Those black coated are from the floor of the said cottages' (21) Sadly Allen's cottages gave way save those sparse mementoes to the modern America Estate. Inhabitants of Bentswood today are privileged though with the knowledge that through William Allen their part of Haywards Heath first came into being as a philanthropic foundation laid from Lindfield years before the arrival of the railway.

William Allen lithograph from drawing by T.F.Dicksee
© Library of the Religious Society of Friends, London

Gravelye Cottages in Allen's America colony late 19th century

JOHN TWISLETON

6 The Cattle Market
Farming past and present

The name Haywards Heath presumes the enclosing of animals. Once the railway station arrived there was the need to supplement enclosure in the area now occupied by Sainsbury's and provide animals with their own railway platform! Turn left out of the station, go under the bridge and you will see the metal gate on the right at the bottom of a rarely used slope where from the mid-1860s to 1989 thousands of stock animals trotted up to carriages to be transported across the country. Upon his death in 1912 Mid Sussex Times provided this obituary of Thomas Bannister who was a key player in opening up the town's importance to farming for over a century: 'Mr. Bannister was born at Cuckfield, his father being a successful agriculturist. Eventually the family moved to Kenward's Farm, near Lindfield, and young Thomas Bannister had for his schoolmaster the late Mr. Thomas Wells. He was a diligent lad. Manual labour did not appeal to him, but intellectual pursuits did. His father permitted him to follow his bent, and on leaving school he was articled to the late Mr. John Agate, an agricultural valuer, who lived at Slaugham. The work interested him, and when he started business on his own account his grip of things and his quick and correct judgement of the qualities of cattle - also of men - speedily gained for him an excellent reputation. It was where the Liverpool Hotel at Haywards Heath now stands [sic] that Mr. Bannister conducted his early auction sales. At that time timber and saw pits were his surroundings. In 1868 he realised the possibilities of a cattle auction mart at Haywards Heath, and although he started in a small way - tradition hath it it was with three sheep penned between three hurdles - yet he was spared to see his early labours fruitful and his market become one of the most important in Sussex for the sale of cattle. First the sales were held monthly, next fortnightly, and then, in response to the general demand, weekly. Mr. Bannister never tired of urging farmers to breed good stock, and those who followed his advice had the satisfaction of obtaining in the auction ring high prices. He himself was never so happy as when upon a farm and inspecting stock, and he was a most successful breeder of pedigree Sussex cattle and large black pigs. For over forty years he acted as agent for the Sergison estate, and most of the sales of building land in Haywards Heath were effected through him. To-day the town has to thank him for the building restrictions he imposed. But for him there would not have been the present nice wide roads and open spaces which make the locality such an attraction to health seekers' (22).

The cattle market became one of the twelve largest in the UK. Held on this side of the railway in different locations the final one is now covered by Sainsbury's car park. About 100,000 stock were sold each year. Residents of Haywards Heath would regularly experience a 'farmyard smell' now unfamiliar to us and processions of animals from Muster Green to market down Boltro Road with its appropriate 'bull trough' association via the old Bulltrowe farm. In 'Haywards Heath - A History & Celebration' (2005) Wilfrid Jackson writes: 'It must be remembered that the present size of Muster Green is approximately just one third of its original area. It was later to be used as a meeting place for the annual get-together of farm labourers from the surrounding estates. Such gatherings are thought to be the origins of the annual Dolphin Fair; this was originally a pig fair, where large numbers of pigs would be temporarily penned to enable everyone to have a good opportunity to scrutinise the animals. The pigs were also allowed to roam within the nearby oak woods, eating acorns. As this was primarily a social gathering, it was not long before travelling tradesmen were selling their wares. Needless to say, refreshments were not discouraged: there are reports of a specific tent erected to cater for the consumption of beer, spirits and bread and cheese. The farms in the immediate neighbourhood were notably Great Haywards and Bulltrowe (later corrupted to Boltro), and were geographically separated by Muster Green. Other local farms were Gravelye, Sugworth, Penland and Harlands, all of which were situated north of Bulltrowe. These latter farms were all connected to the Burrell family to a greater or lesser degree, and were all to be affected by the arrival of the railway. Getting around would entail following tracks that in summer would be dusty and dry, yet muddy and wet during the winter months. The roads were generally very difficult and sometimes dangerous to use, and were no doubt impassable sometimes. The farms hereabouts were fairly extensive, as they generally concentrated on the grazing of animals, thus avoiding the need to till the heavy clay soil' (23).

For over a century Bannister's Livestock Market provided a hub for farming in and around Haywards Heath served also by the Station Hotel, bank and garage whose buildings remain. Sue Perkins née Allen recalls: 'I grew up in Queens Road in the black and white houses at the top of the road. Tuesday was Market day and as a little girl I can remember standing at the front gate watching the farmers driving their cattle up the road to the Market situated where Sainsbury's Supermarket now stands. Haywards Heath Market was the central hub for all farmers in the outlying villages in Mid Sussex'. The original lands of Bulltrowe Farm (also Boltro) now host the main civic buildings of Haywards Heath including the Town Hall and main Council buildings.

Another feature of the former town hub tracing back to the seventeenth century was the corn mill serving farmers bringing grain to town to be made into flour. Jenner & Higgs Mill started 1856 sited on Balcombe Road south of the railway station with a water wheel then reputedly the largest in the country. This was eventually supplemented as many mills were by a steam engine fired by a Tangye gas fire installed when gas arrived about 1887. In 1915 Haywards Heath saw drama as the mill store at the Railway Station was completely burned down. It was thought that a spark from a passing Railway Engine ignited in the four storey hay store. This happened over the lunch hour so by the time the fire was discovered it had such a great hold all that could be done was to save the adjoining property. With the demolition of the chimney and filling in of the mill pond by the railway bridge in 1969 there is no trace of the old mill today whose grounds are covered by the Barnmead estate off Balcombe Road.

Farming today around Haywards Heath presents, as ever, a mixed picture with the varied soil types and lay of the land. Unlike other English counties Sussex still has a healthy mix of livestock production, arable and dairy.

Haywards Heath Corn Mill buildings by the station railway bridge demolished 1969

Bannisters Livestock Market c1930 from Smith's 'Haywards Heath in old picture postcards' (1993).

JOHN TWISLETON

7 Place of therapy
The Asylum and hospitals

'It was gratifying to see the pale London patients getting a bit of colour in their cheeks and generally benefitting from the pure air and water of Haywards Heath. The beauty also of the site of the asylum looking out over the downs, which ever changing their distance and their shape, as the light and cloud shadows sail over them has not been without its calming influence on many of the patients' (24). So wrote the first medical superintendent, Dr Lockhart Robertson after the arrival of the first inmates of Sussex County Asylum, later known as St Francis Hospital, in 1859 drawn partially from the notorious Bethnal Green (Bedlam) Asylum. In 1854 the Government had made it obligatory that each county should make provision for its mentally afflicted poor and the opening of the railway made Haywards Heath the obvious choice. The design submitted by the architect H.E.Kendall had been accepted in 1856, an Italianate style with different coloured bricks, flanked by two bell towers, on a ridge overlooking the South Downs purposely chosen for its airy position to serve the health of the patients. 'It included accommodation for 420 inmates plus offices, superintendent's apartments, chapel, lodge, stable, gas works, baths, showers, brewhouse and washrooms. An artesian well 217 ft deep supplied water and still does today [evidenced by the great Water Tower] ... by 1861, the female inmates were able to make most of the garments required. The domestic work was also carried out by inmates and many men worked on the farm. However, 16 artisans were employed and it was part of their duties to instruct inmates. The term 'artisan' covered such diverse occupations as tailors, shoemakers, carpenters, bakers, painters, bricklayers, glaziers and mat makers. With farm and garden produce and self-sufficiency in the workshops, the Asylum was most economically run... The everyday fare was meat, soup, mutton broth and potatoes - occasionally cheese would be served with milk from the farm and bread baked on the premises. In the early years 33 attendants (17 male and 16 female) provided custodial care only; looking after personal hygiene, behaviour and occupation: inmates had to be supervised. For example, before they left the dining hall all cutlery was counted to prevent the possibility of injury, and only then were the inmates allowed to leave. Initially one male and one female member of staff patrolled overnight, but eventually each ward had a night attendant whose wakefulness was monitored, not only by the night superintendent, but also by electric pegging clocks, on which a key had to be turned every hour to prove he/she was not asleep. The concept of a social life for the inmates was an integral part of the asylum... their amusement. The important Victorian values of discipline and industry were essential to good order and rehabilitation... Fraternisation between male and female staff was strictly forbidden and the subject of fines and even being asked to leave. Dr Robertson wrote in 1867: 'This is a hospital for the treatment of disease not a matrimonial agency'. The female staff were allowed to take the air in the kitchen garden whilst the male staff were confined to the sports fields!' (25)

The Asylum Arms, Haywards Heath appeared in 1857 among 20 temporary buildings erected to serve the 200 workers building the Sussex County Asylum. The Arms run by James Ashdown offered 'very neat and commodious liquor' according to the Brighton Examiner of 2 June 1857. The pub was situated on the

Asylum Road (now Colwell Road) junction with Sussex Road (now Wivelsfield Road). Demolished before 1874 Asylum Arms' coming and going is a reminder of how the elongated shape of Haywards Heath derives from the construction of the County Hospital to its south with its large population, staff, pastoral and commercial significance. The decision to build at such a distance from the station was linked to the Victorian understanding of mental disability.

Treatment of mental illness in Victorian times differs so much from our day with isolation seen as the key for fear of contamination with asylum inmates kept in remote, secure institutions so as to separate them from the populace as a whole. Haywards Heath Asylum nevertheless broke new ground in treating mental illness through pioneer Doctor Lockhart Robertson who used vapour baths to soothe his patients, the beginning of a more optimistic and therapeutic approach to mental illness. The story of the asylum now converted into the apartments at Southdowns Park is told in 'Sweet bells jangled out of tune' by James Gardner (1999) and 'My Asylum' by Joe Hughes (2015).

'Not everything about the Sussex Asylum in the early days was negative. Indeed, many of the principles implemented by Robertson and other reformers are re-emerging again today: the recognition of the value of a good diet; the need to build on patients' strengths rather than their weaknesses; the importance of a patient being ready for rehabilitation (as shown by Robertson's flexible policy over discharge); and encouraging patients to widen their capabilities by giving them a diverse range of activities; and above all the importance of kindness as a basis for treatment... Looking at the Sussex Asylum we can see how much physical space was important to a patient's well being. Even though the labyrinth of corridors - totalling more than a mile - were depressing places, they did afford patients an opportunity to walk out their anxiety however bad the weather was outside. The asylum also offered patients: occupation, companionship and... giving the patients a high level of protection and security. All these are rights that may be more difficult to guarantee in a wider society. Lastly, life in the asylum was an experience shared by staff and patients alike. Many of the former lived in the same grounds, used the same facilities... for them, it was not just a job, it was a vocational interest. They worked in an environment that encouraged a certain amount of befriending and friendship, concepts that, with all the boundaries of today's caring professions, may be difficult to maintain. If community care is to succeed surely it must capture some of the spirit the best asylum workers demonstrated in the past. Although the Sussex Asylum (or St Francis) is no more, its main building still dominates the landscape. It is, at present (1999), being converted into luxury housing - 'its developer coyly disguising its stigmatising past" (26). With the arrival of the National Health Service in 1948 the Asylum became known as St Francis Hospital which came eventually under the oversight of Princess Royal Hospital (1991) closing 1995. The Princess Royal standing on the same ridge chosen 1856 is itself now overseen as part of University Hospitals Sussex. This broad brush town history should at least give mention of King Edward VII and Eliot Memorial Hospital (1912), the cottage hospital formerly on Butlers Green Road. This closed in the 1990s but land nearby still hosts the town's NHS mental health services.

St. Francis Hospital Haywards Heath.

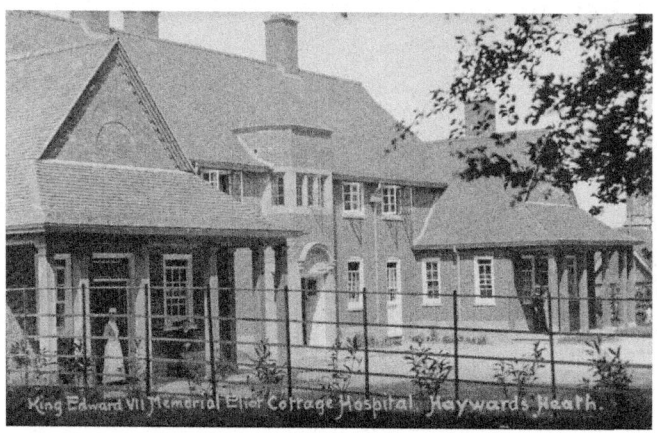

King Edward VII Memorial Eliot Cottage Hospital, Haywards Heath.

JOHN TWISLETON

8   **Enterprising hub**
Commuter town

My first sight of Haywards Heath though unknowing was as a child viewing BBC Children's Television where a popular feature for young and old was *London to Brighton in Four Minutes* a speeded up version of the hour long journey from London Victoria to Brighton viewed from the driver's cab produced in 1953. Years later 4 January 1967 living in Settle near the Lake District I recall as a teenager news on TV of the fatal crash of racing entrepreneur Donald Campbell nearby in Coniston Water whilst attempting to break the water speed record. On our move to Haywards Heath in 2001 I quickly learned of Campbell's association with the town through his partnership in pioneering work on jet engines including *Bluebird K7* with Lew and Ken Norris. The three have a plaque at the former Norris House in Burrell Road and I have met older residents of that area who recall letters apologising for jet noise when the hydroplane was tested in 1966. More recently on TV, from day to day, I see the contemporary Quiz Presenter and author Richard Osman, a celebrity with roots in Cuckfield and Haywards Heath who attended Warden Park School. I describe this book as a broad brush celebration of Haywards Heath framed by myself but with an eye to significant milestones, entrepreneurs and personalities. People like stories and as a writer my best effort has been to present a weaving together of local knowledge that catches the eye as to my mind does the enterprising spirit of the railway, Campbell and Osman.

Alongside builder Richard Pannett and auctioneer Thomas Bannister leading late 19th century town entrepreneurs already celebrated, Wilfred Jackson praises the actress Amy Sedgwick (1830-1897) buried in St Wilfrid's Churchyard and styled 'The Queen of Comedy' who enthralled Queen Victoria on the London stage but was extremely popular at the Theatre Royal, Brighton. The legacy of James Bradford (1840-1930) who made his money from the railway and bought Oaklands, built by Brighton bookseller Harry Treacher, is seen in the Almshouses bearing his name he built in 1912 which still serve the population today. Jesse Finch worked with Frederick Beeny to develop and build houses along Mill Green Road and College Road at the turn of the 19th century. Charles Clarke (1841-1921) came to Haywards Heath around 1871 already interested in establishing his own newspaper business. 'He set up his printing press in New Road, then just a rough and muddy track, near the railway station - New Road would later be called Boltro Road. Charles had the foresight to see that the railway was already attracting several businesses to the town, all of which, big or small, would need to advertise their services. He soon established links with many of the local businesses... producing the first local directory in 1879, listing both businesses and prominent private residences. Businesses were happy to advertise their services. The directory was extremely popular, and cost 2d. Its success gave Charles the opportunity to start a weekly newspaper. He was widely supported throughout the community, ranging from official bodies such as the Local Board, the Church, and the Sussex Asylum, to the fledgling businesses that were trading locally. The residents were also very supportive - the local newspaper would certainly create a community spirit. In 1881, with the help of his family, he produced the first edition of The Mid Sussex Times. Costing one penny, it consisted of four pages of news that had been printed in London, which Clarke added to a further four pages of advertising and local news that had been both reported and printed by himself. He was both reporter and editor in the very early days, but it would soon become apparent that he would need assistance, and he therefore started to employ a team of skilled workers' (27). Conway Gabe co-author of the substantive history of Haywards Heath 1981 and a later editor of 'The Middy' notes the wider contribution Clarke made to town life: 'It was written of him: "No man was better known in the district than he, and no man had fewer enemies. His great desire was to be helpful to others ... Of the paper he called into being he was justly proud, and to those who were responsible for its production he was always considerate and kind".... For his funeral service, the Congregational Church in South Road, Haywards Heath, was filled to overflowing. For 40 years he had been a stalwart of the Congregational cause in the town... a deacon and for much of the time church secretary... for 26 years he was superintendent of the Sunday School. A member of the Institute of Journalists, Charles Clarke was also a director of Haywards Heath and District Building Society and The Mid Sussex Permanent Building Society, and in the 1870s he was secretary of Haywards Heath Cricket Club... Haywards Heath Cottage Hospital, the local Horticultural Society and the Cuckfield Agricultural Association also claimed his support. To Charles Clarke was credited the initiation of a movement for a fire protection service in Mid Sussex. He was responding to the toast of "The Press" at a Burgess Hill festive gathering, when he suggested the formation of a fire brigade for the protection of lives and property in the neighbourhood. The idea was quickly taken up and resulted in the formation of The Burgess Hill and Mid Sussex Fire Brigade. Other brigades were afterwards formed for the towns and villages of Mid Sussex (28). In 1882 cabinet-maker George Hilton from Hastings made a timely arrival in Haywards Heath from Hastings when so many houses were being built. 'George Hilton & Sons' furnishings shop on South Road, built 1932, continued until its site became part of Orchards shopping precinct in 1982. A second Hilton's across the road is now Dyas's. Cigarette manufacturer William Yapp, a most successful businessman, lived at Beech Hurst and after his death in 1946 left the house and gardens to the town. These remain with their miniature railway and scenic view of the South Downs, a favourite for family outings locally through Yapp's philanthropy. The curly gutter brackets on several houses in Haywards Heath are the trademark of enterprising architect Harold Turner (1885-1961) born in Ardingly who in 1930 set up his practice in the town. Turner's most notable project was designing Franklands Village in the mid 1930s at the invitation of the Rotary Club which provided inexpensive housing for young couples. Enterprising people like those aforementioned are servants of social change. Haywards Heath has been blessed over its years as a hub of enterprise not least through commuting entrepreneurs exercising their gifts in London, Sussex and through Gatwick across the world, some of whom have left an enduring legacy in their home town of Haywards Heath.

Donald Campbell with Bluebird on Burrell Road 1966

Clarke's Local Directory advertisements 1879 reproduced in Ford & Gabe's Metropolis 1981

JOHN TWISLETON

9   **Schooling and recreation**
Education, sports and leisure

The original St Wilfrid's School, now Zizzi's restaurant, next to the Church was a hub of activity twice daily for almost a century from its building in 1857. As horse and cart gave way to the motor car it became a dangerous site for pedestrians so that the school was moved to Eastern Road in 1951. The old site sits on the traffic hub we call the gyratory instead of the human 'hub' it once was with families across the town converging upon it daily on foot. In its early days the school curriculum included teaching the boys the art of rifle shooting, a skill helpful to their later participation in soldiery. The elementary school - rivalled by several private schools - was complemented by the provision in 1907 of a secondary school nearby in South Road. Now demolished, this was replaced in 1938 by Oathall School, a new building on the boundary between Haywards Heath and Lindfield. This secondary modern school would have been initially inundated with children evacuated to the town from London to escape bombing in the 1939-1945 World War. Charles Tucker describes the arrival of the grammar school now Haywards Heath College: 'With relatives living in College Road I spent many hours of my childhood playing in the grounds of Harlands Farm. I would walk along College Road under the railway bridge and pass the two ponds which served Jenner & Higgs Mill then down a footpath into Packham's fields where we would have family picnics among the haystacks. This all ended in 1957 when the fields were acquired to build the grammar school that I attended a few years later. Building the school was halted for a time when it was found to be going on across an ancient bridle path that had to be officially diverted. We had to walk through the building whilst permission was obtained to divert the path. The rest of Harlands Farm disappeared under the developments we know as Harlands Estate, Barnmead and Burrell Road Light Industrial Estate'. In this broad brush celebration of Haywards Heath schools mention should more briefly be made of Harlands, Northlands Wood, Bolnore Village, Warden Park and St Joseph's primary schools, the latter complemented by St Paul's Catholic College, which moved in 2004 to Burgess Hill, as well as numerous private schools. The name of one of these, St Clair's, a girls' school established about 1935 now defunct, was preserved by popular choice for the entertainment complex Clair Hall built upon its former grounds off Perrymount Road and opened in 1974.

Reflecting on the history of football in Haywards Heath Mike Lewis writes of unique problems emerging for games on Muster Green as the town grew: 'In 1894 a complaint was made to the Local Board that "unfortunately for vehicular traffic, the sport is starting to have a tendency to frighten horses". The Middy waxes lyrical about the Muster Green, observing that "Haywards Heath is one of the few towns which maintains what practically amounts to a village green in its midst, unaffected by the onward march of bricks and mortar. In summer months it is used for cricket, while in winter football reigns supreme over its surface".' (29) The first football match played by a team representing Haywards Heath was in March 1888. In 1895 'The Bluebells' with their blue and white colours gained use of Richard Pannett's meadow, the field in South Road later to become Victoria Park, using the then adjacent fire station as changing rooms. In 1952 through the hard work of the Supporters' Club Hanbury Park Stadium opened with 3,000 spectators to see their team play Horsham when the visitors won 1-0. The title 'Haywards Heath Football Club' was adopted during the centenary year of 1988 and during the 1990s there was a name change to 'The Blues'. The Women's Team, linked to Crawley Wasps, started to play home matches at Hanbury from the 2023/24 season (30).

Haywards Heath Cricket Club was founded 1897 once local entrepreneur Jesse Finch had sorted the fouled, boggy water course and funds had been raised to lay turf on Heath Recreation Ground (Clair Meadow) to mark Queen Victoria's Diamond Jubilee. The cricket pavilion was opened in 1900. One of the players in the first match on the new ground, Fred Tate was for a time landlord of the adjacent Burrell Arms. His son Maurice outshone him as a cricketer. 'Maurice rendered his county and his country great service in the 1920s as a batsman and particularly as a bowler. He played with distinction in Test matches at home and overseas... Seven times Maurice Tate scored 1,000 runs or more and took 100 wickets or more in a season (31). Haywards Heath Tennis Club traces back to 1898 when William Fry gave use of his garden at Ellensleigh, Boltro Road for tennis. In 1909 the Club successfully sought provision of courts in Victoria Park, later converted into hard courts to enable year-round play. Haywards Heath Rugby and Golf Clubs operate outside town. Haywards Heath & Beech Hurst Bowls Club, as its name indicates, is linked to William Yapp's gift of Beech Hurst to the town.

Peter Miles writes: 'Haywards Heath's romance with the cinema lasted for sixty years, three picturehouses in total, the first of these being The Heath in The Broadway which showed silent black and white films to the accompaniment of the piano for atmospheric effect. In the 1930s competition with two new and more modern cinemas brought about its closure. The Broadway (1932) and The Perrymount (1936) brought a new level of entertainment to the town. The Broadway, with its attractive decor and stalls and circle seating, was popular with the showing of Hollywood and British films on larger screen size with sound typical of the new age of filmgoing. The Perrymount, situated off Commercial Square, was a large building, complete with cinema, dance hall and restaurant. In the post war years both of the town's cinemas proved popular entertainment venues, showing Musicals, Comedy and Drama Thrillers, also Children's Matinee shows on Saturday mornings. Sadly, The Broadway closed in 1954 but The Perrymount continued successfully until 1972. Its closure did not take place without protest from the public, a sad time for filmgoers, the end of an era' (32).

Public buildings for recreational use have included the Sussex Hall (1889) which stood where Poundlands now stands, the Library (1961), Clair Hall (1974), Dolphin Leisure Centre (1976) and The Orchards precinct (1982). Charles Tucker recalls 'The Sussex or Public Hall was used for many civic events as well as catering for troops in two world wars. It was also a temporary hospital during World War One. My memories growing up are of being taken to the Sussex Hall by my parents where you would queue in order to get bargains at the many jumble sales held there. We also attended pantomimes put on by the Weald Theatre group amongst others as well as events hosted by the local Vera Sutton School of Dancing. As a teenager in the 60s I clearly remember attending many Saturday night dances in the

Sussex Hall and seeing some little known groups who went on to be famous such as Genesis and Marmalade' (33).

No. 3 St. Wilfrid's Church Schools, Hayward's Heath

JOHN TWISLETON

10   **Spiritual mecca**
Religion and tourism

Looking south from higher ground in the centre of Haywards Heath on a clear day you capture a spiritually entrancing view which has been and remains a draw for many. 'It is remarkable how these South Downs have impressed different observers. E. Hallam Moorhouse wrote that "It is the Downs that... away from Sussex one remembers last and longest." To Gilbert White they were "a chain of majestic mountains." Hilaire Belloc considers them "The spine of the county". They were Swinburne's "green, smooth-swelling, unending Downs". George Eliot called them "those grand, steadfast forms." Harrison Ainsworth said that "No hills can be more beautiful than these South Downs." Galsworthy affirmed that they were "the noblest, the most serene, the most individual, and.. the most spiritual feature in all English scenery" (34).

Through that collection of sayings Albert Gregory celebrates the glory of Mid Sussex which links to how, once built up as a town, Haywards Heath drew a number of religious communities from London and beyond who saw the benefit of isolation with a spiritual intent in such lovely surroundings recently made accessible. In the late nineteenth century the Church of England experienced a movement of prayer and service linked to the recovery of the Church's Catholic rooting not fully disowned at the Reformation. The building of St Wilfrid's Church 1863-5 was influenced by this movement championed by East Grinstead priest John Mason Neale whose sisters donated decorative windows to the new Church. The Community of the Holy Cross was an Anglican religious order founded in 1857 by

Neale's sister Elizabeth at the invitation of Father Charles Lowder, to work with the poor around St Peter's London Docks in Wapping. In 1886 the Community bought land on Bolnore Road and the foundation stone of Holy Cross Convent was blessed by Father Richard Benson SSJE in 1887. Lord Halifax laid the foundation stone of the Chapel in 1902. The sisters continued work in Haywards Heath with orphans and young girls. In 1926 the full Latin, Benedictine daily prayer or Office was embraced. Eventually the community changed from being an active to a more contemplative community providing retreats and quiet days. By the 1970s the Community was much reduced in numbers so in 1977 the decision was made to move to a smaller Convent in Rempstone near Loughborough. The Convent cemetery remains as a fenced off island in Bolnore woods. Exploiting the beauty of the town's surroundings, the former Chichester Diocesan conference and retreat house, Elfinsward, stood near Holy Rood Convent at the top of Bolnore Road. Donated by Mrs Gerald Moor 1928 it was sold in 1973 to Sussex Police. In 1886 a Roman Catholic community of Belgian sisters established The Priory of Our Lady of Good Counsel with a school for girls on Franklynn Road. The Priory Chapel (1891) remains the most prominent feature of Haywards Heath supplemented by St Paul's Church opened in 1930. Peter Miles recalls the rather severe dominance of the walled Convent near the town centre in the 1960s with the occasional appearance of one nun pushing another around in a wheelchair. Having dwindled in numbers the community relinquished the Priory in 1977 heading to Sayers Common. The walls came down to serve local housing development and the Priory now converted into flats remains a notable feature on the skyline of Haywards Heath still pointing heavenwards.

Wyn Ford's 'The Church in Sussex Road' (1994) chronicles the rise and fall of the Primitive Methodist congregation started in 1876. With an emphasis away from set services upon Holy Spirit inspired free prayer, Primitive Methodism appealed to 'the lowly working classes of English society' (Ford). It became a school of oratory for many leaders in the Trades Union movement. 'The preaching of the free grace of God' was stated as the motive for London District opening a Wesleyan Chapel for Haywards Heath on Perrymount Road in 1900. First minister Revd Bennett, a Cornishman experienced as a Church builder, prepared the way by gathering a congregation. Though Primitive and Wesleyan Methodists formally united in 1932 Sussex Road continued separately until 1991 when its congregation joined Perrymount Road Methodists handing their building over to the Baptist Church which was rebuilt in 2017. The town's strict Baptist Church dates back to 1879 when the Congregationalists, now part of the United Reformed Church and Primitive Methodists were cited in the town directory as 'principal places of worship' alongside St Wilfrid's (35). The parish Church planted four daughter churches starting in 1882 with the Presentation Church in Bentswood paid for by Mary Otter, initially a prefabricated iron clad structure. St Richard's Church on Sydney Road started 1897 as the Chapel of the Holy Spirit. Ascension Chapel was erected 1895 in St John's Road. This was demolished and the congregation re-sited at the former Congregational Church in Wivelsfield Road, renamed St Edmund's Church, moving on with their old name to the current Ascension Church built 1966 in Vale Road. The fourth Anglican Church plant was the Church of the Good Shepherd serving Franklands Village from 1964-5 until its closure in 2002. That year saw the foundation of the town's Ruwach Pentecostal Church. Earlier a group of Pentecostals met first locally in 1977 becoming the New Frontiers affiliated Kings Church Mid-Sussex 2005 and moving 2012 to Burgess Hill. In 1967 the Evangelical Free Church known now as Christ Church was built in New England Road where it had possessed a hall since 1936. Haywards Heath Mosque also known as Mid-Sussex Islamic Centre opened 2010 in the old St Edmund's Church serving local people, many from Muslim countries overseas recruited to serve the town's hospital and residential homes.

Though Haywards Heath draws people into the town's service industries it is employment-wise primarily a commuter town serving Brighton & Hove, Crawley, Gatwick Airport and London. The town is also attractive for its situation as witnessed by the early wave of religious foundations into Haywards Heath seeking space for the spirit in the countryside made accessible by the railway. Parallel to this are contemporary tourists who see Haywards Heath as an attractive venue providing easy access to the beauty of Mid Sussex and the south coast as well as the vibrancy of London. This book brings onto paper many of the reflections shared on 'Haywards Heath in days gone by' Facebook Group. It looks to the day when another more solid provision will be made to help celebrate the town's history through hosting and volunteers servicing a Haywards Heath Museum.

'Celebrating Haywards Heath: Heart of Sussex' is primarily an outline of the riches of the town. The main part of the book ends with a commendation of its secondary provision, the Appendices with rail routes to sights in Sussex and London from Haywards Heath station. These complement the author's earlier work 'Fifty Walks from Haywards Heath' serving discovery nearer to hand.

Priory Convent farm off Western Road early 20th century

Fr Thomas Wyatt (left) laid the foundation stone of St Richard's blessed by the Bishop of Lewes (centre) 5 September 1937

JOHN TWISLETON

Postscript

St Wilfrid's School project

In 2019 Haywards Heath Town Team formed up a local history project engaging young people looking towards a series of talks, dramatic presentations and exhibitions linked to Town Day 2020. Local schools, youth clubs and uniformed organisations began to welcome visits from local historians to form up plans. This project, including Town Day itself, was cancelled due to the COVID 19 Lockdown.

Five years on following conversations with Haywards Heath Town Council the author served a plan to resume a cross-generational celebration of town history by approaching St Wilfrid's Church of England Primary School in the late autumn of 2023. In early 2024 their Head, Simon Hateley met with Fr John Twisleton and invited him to present an interactive talk on Haywards Heath to Year 6 children. The author worked with Year 6 teachers Adam Belton and Dee MacTaggart in preparing the 30 children to interview 18 people who had mostly lived in Haywards Heath all of their lives as part of St Richard's Church weekday church hall hospitality, Ric's Bench.

On 12 June 2024 the parish priest Fr David King welcomed the children along with John Junior Delaney, Clem Frank, Daphne Griffin, Brenda Heald, Tony Heald, Joe Hughes, Anne Jones, Mary King, Joy Madgwick, Peter Miles, David Pidgeon, Patrick Robey, Charles Tucker, Dave Tucker, Nicole Tucker, Louise Wagger, Melvyn Walmsley and Chris Whitehead. For just over an hour the children interviewed the latter about their best memories of Haywards Heath, the biggest changes they had seen and what they thought the future holds for the town assisted by a timeline of local events prepared by the author. The children brought pencil and paper to take notes with an eye to recording the most interesting things that came up in their conversations. The author was given sight of these notes from which some of the main lines recorded are condensed below.

Nelly P's notes on **Dave and Nicole Tucker**'s interview:

Dave heard the Doodlebug landing in Western Road (1944) when he was at school in Lindfield. They recall flats and houses being built and the high street changing and remember the fields where they used to play during the war. As children on the holidays on a Tuesday they would go inside the Cattle Market and sometimes there would be a Sunday Market. Sainsburys was where Poundland is. The first cinema was where Côte is. The Post Office was opposite the Library. They remember Donald Campbell's Bluebird and when they built it. They remember big processions of Brownies and Cubs. Iceland was originally called British Restaurant, then the Youth club. A storm made a tree fall on someone's house. Fire station used to be the gas works. Under Haywards Heath station the corn and wheat store once caught fire.

Serhii's notes on **Joe Hughes** interview:

Moved to Haywards Heath in 1967 while 18 years old. Best time 1970-1980 when the town was thriving. Noticed the disappearance of many supermarkets and there being not so many shops. Biggest change to him was the closing of Saint Francis Hospital 1859-1995. Favourite place is the Haywards

Heath library. Would like to see funding for a museum where St Francis Hospital was.

Olivia H's notes on **Anne Jones** interview:

I loved going to the cattle market and seeing it was amazing. I loved the fact that there were so many things to do. We had three cinemas. Haywards Heath used to be smaller and more welcoming. I was there for the opening of the Dolphin in 1976. Princess Royal Hospital opened in 1991 and I was there and got to see Princess Anne. I helped the fight to keep the Accident & Emergency unit. We don't have enough hospitals, care homes and educational provision. My husband went to where Zizzis is for school where St Wilfrid's used to be. In the war there was a German prisoner taken to the hospital to use his skills to save lives. I was a governor of Warden Park primary. My husband's friend killed ducks and sold them and cut down trees and sold them. Boys ran wild with fathers away in the war. A ten year old boy was found near some lemonade bottles with smoke coming out of his head. The Military Police were called and he was driven to the Cottage Hospital where he was plunged in a bath of water with only his nose exposed. The bottles were Molotov Cocktails and he was shaking them! I remember a man called Jack who used to be in the old Ugly Duckling Pub. He would sit there swearing at people. I spoke to him and found out he was nice but he had brain damage and was a patient at St Francis Psychiatric Hospital. We now have more churches than pubs as many have closed. I was sad we didn't keep the cinema and a lot of things have changed because there was no one fighting for them. The only places we can build on are our lovely green spaces but we need to keep these.

Evie P and Nellie K's notes on **Tony Heald** interview:

When he first lived in Western Road there was only one car. The Dolphin was raising money for Garden centres. When you shopped in Sainsburys there would be different counters: cheese, milk, bread, yoghurt and chocolate. Oathall farm used to just be a place to garden. When the war was on people slept and lived in a metal cage which was in the living room in case a bomb fell. The doodle bug, one fell on the town in 1944, had an engine to alert that it was nearby. When it stopped that meant it had dropped. It cost 2 and a half pence to get in the Cinema on Broadway. Sainsburys used to be on South Road, then where Poundland is, and eventually located where it is currently.

Kara and Jake's notes on **Mary King** interview:

Pilgrim Pub - bands played underneath - where Morrisons is. Donald Campbell built land speed record holding vehicle Bluebird in Burrell Road 1966. Presentation Hall used to be built out of wood and corrugated iron but got burnt down 1979. Cattle Market closed in 1989 and is now Sainsbury's. There was a Sunday market. They closed Haywards Heath Hospital opposite Beechhurst. Bolnore Village used to be fields. Haywards Heath didn't have a bypass but started where Bolnore Village is. They built the bypass before Bolnore Village. The Mosque which opened 2010 used to be a Church of England Church (St Edmund's) which closed down because there weren't many people. Waitrose used to be Haywards Heath bus station. Haywards Heath railway station is here because Lindfield and Cuckfield didn't want a railway station. There used to be a swimming pool at the Birch Hotel, Oathall Community College and St Wilfrid's School. We need more swimming pools. Be good to improve the Dolphin. Sad Clair Hall not being used, it needs refurbishing or replacing. Too many coffee shops and hairdressers but not enough for people to do. We need a better skate park, more facilities.

Isabelle's notes on **Daphne Griffin** interview:

Daphne likes reading - her favourite book genre is history. Her favourite memory is having little shops around the town. When the hospital changed location is her least favourite memory. Knocking down Hiltons to build Orchards was the biggest change. She used to sell flowers at Muster Green - still does. Her first impression of Haywards Heath was bad, it was boring so she moved to Cuckfield. She moved back and now prefers it. Remembers seeing Donald Campbell who prepared his speed boat in Burrell Road on TV.

Henry S's notes on **Charles Tucker** interview:

Charles was a police officer in Haywards Heath from 1980-1987 then he was promoted and had to go to Crawley. He likes golf, squash and football. Three favourite memories are of the Cattle Market, Perrymount Cinema and Dolphin Fair. Thinks there are too many cars in Haywards Heath. Remembers going down to the Pilgrim pub and being caught by his parents. Very sad about losing the fields. Thinks Haywards Heath will continue to get bigger and bigger. Remembers the Dolphin Leisure Centre opening, going down to the cinema at Perrymount Rd and walking down Clair Park. He would like a cinema in town and more community spirit.

It is hoped that St Wilfrid's School project will catalyse other local schools to engage with long term residents about their memories and aspirations for Haywards Heath.

'Ric's Bench' in St Richard's Church Hall, Sydney Road with St Wilfrid's Church of England School Year 6 pupils and teachers, interviewees, parish priest Fr David King and Fr John Twisleton on Wednesday 12 June 2024

Timeline

1261	Place name 'Hayworth' first recorded
1638	Fine map of local sites published
1642	Battle of Haywards Heath in English Civil War associated with Muster Green
1827	Philanthropist William Allen publishes 'Colonies at Home' pamphlet preparatory to opening his allotment colony
1841	Opening of Haywards Heath railway station
1846	Corn stores erected. Corn market every Wednesday at the Corn Exchange adjoining the Station Hotel.
1857	St Wilfrid's School established on South Road
1859	Opening of Sussex Lunatic Asylum (St Francis' Hospital)
1859	Opening of Bannister's Cattle Market closed 1989
1863f	Opening of St Wilfrid's Church
1866	Gas works by the railway station
1882	Mission Room predecessor of Presentation Church. Brick building completed 1897
1886	Building of the Priory of Our Lady. Sisters leave for Sayers Common 1977
1886	Presentation Church opened through gift of philanthropist Mary Otter
1887	Victoria Recreation Ground designated on Queen Victoria's Golden Jubilee
1911	First cinema, Heath Theatre in The Broadway.
1917	Western Road Cemetery opens as overflow from St Wilfrid's Churchyard
1921	Haywards Heath United Services Club
1924	First Council Houses at top of New England Rd - 50 at Woodlands Rd & Mayflower Rd

1930s	Electrification of railway led to changes in Commercial Square
1932	Broadway Cinema at top of Perrymount Rd
1933	Rotary Club begins Franklands Village construction to Harold Turner's design
1936	Perrymount Cinema & Dance Hall erected in Commercial Square area
1936	Haywards Heath Evangelical Free Church
1938	Oathall College opens
1938	St Richard's Church consecrated by Bishop George Bell
1939f	Oathall Community College Farm founded to help the war effort
1944	11 July flying bomb (Doodlebug) fell in woods at the back of Western Road Cemetery.
1951	St Wilfrid's School moves from South Road to Eastern Road
1951	The Pilgrim Pub opened in 1951 named after William Allen with a picture of a Pilgrim father on the pub sign.
1951/2	Woodside Cottages demolished
1966	Donald Campbell's *Bluebird* tested Burrell Road. Campbell's fatal crash 1967
1971	Queen Elizabeth II visits the International HQ of the Royal Commonwealth Society For The Blind, now Sightsavers.
1976	The Dolphin Leisure Centre opened
1979	Presentation Hall burnt and rebuilt 1983
1981	Cuckfield Museum opened as a resource for Cuckfield and Haywards Heath
1982	Orchards shopping precinct opened
1991	Princess Royal Hospital opened by Princess Anne
2002	First house opened in Bolnore Village

2010 Haywards Heath Mosque opened in former Ascension/St Edmund's Church building
2014 Haywards Heath by-pass/relief road opened for A272. Town rd named B2272.
2018 Jack Hayward legendary highwayman restored 1950s sign erected Heath Rd

JOHN TWISLETON

Index

A272	16, 17, 18, 19
Abbots Leigh House	17
Allen, William	12, 34-38
America Estate	35-37, 100
Ascension Church & Chapel	66
Asylum Arms	47-48
Bannister, Thomas	30, 40, 42, 44, 52
Baptist Church	66
Barnmead Estate	43
Battle of Haywards Heath	29
Beech Hurst	55, 60
Bentswood	12-13
Birch Hotel	73
Bodley, George	31
Bolnore Garden Village	16, 73
Bolnore Village Primary School	59
Bradford, James	53
British Restaurant	71
Broadway Cinema	61
Bulltrowe (Boltro) Farm	42
Burrell Arms	30
Burrell Family	12, 30
Butler's Green House	28
Campbell, Donald	52, 71, 73, 74
Cattle Market	23, 30, 40, 41, 42, 43, 71, 72, 74,
Clair Hall	61, 74
Clarke, Charles	53
Congregationalist Church	11

Cooper, Revd James	31
Corn Mill	43-44, 71
Dinnage's Garage ('Pennies')	28
Dolphin Fair	41, 74
Dolphin Leisure Centre	28, 30, 61, 72, 74
Dolphin Pub aka Sergison Arms	28
Elfinsward	65
Finch, Jesse	53
Good Shepherd Church	66
Great Haywards Farm	28, 42
Hanbury Park Stadium	59
Harlands Farm	42, 58, 59
Harlands Primary School	59
Hayward, Jack (Highwayman)	30
Haywards Heath	
College (Grammar School)	58
Cricket Club	54, 60
Football Club	59, 60
Golf Club	60
Horticultural Society	54
Rotary Club	12, 55
Rugby Club	60
Town Hall	43
Hayworth Enclosure	11, 12, 14, 28
Heath Cinema	60, 62
High Weald	12, 17
Hilton, George	55, 74
Holy Cross Convent	64, 65
Kendall, H.E.	46
King Edward & Eliot Memorial Hospital	49, 50, 73
Library	61, 72

Liverpool Arms	23, 24, 26, 40
Middy or Mid Sussex Times	53-54, 59
Morris, William	31
Mosque	63, 73
Muster Green	28-29, 41, 59
Neale, John Mason	32, 64-65
Norris, Lew & Ken	52
Northlands Wood Primary School	59
Oathall School	58, 73
Orchards Precinct	61
Osman, Richard	52
Pannett, Richard	30, 52
Perrymount Cinema	61, 74
Perrymount Road Methodist Church	66
Pilgrim Pub	37, 73
Premier Inn	24
Presentation Church	13, 73, 100-105
Primitive Methodist Church	11, 66
Princess Royal Hospital	49, 72
Priory Chapel & Convent	13, 65
Robertson, Dr Lockhart	46, 47
Ruwach Pentecostal Church	67
Sedgwick, Amy	53
Sergison Family	12, 28, 30-32, 41
Slugwash Lane	17
Star Hotel	31
Station Inn	24, 28
Steeple Cottage	28
St Clair's School	59
St Edmund's Church	66-67, 73
St Francis Hospital formerly Asylum	12, 46, 50, 72

St Joseph's Primary School	59
St Paul's Catholic College	59
St Richard's Church	66, 68, 70
St Wilfrid's Church	11, 13, 20, 30
St Wilfrid's Primary School	31, 58, 70-75
Sussex Hall aka Public Hall	61-62
Turner, Harold	55
United Reformed Church	66
Vera Sutton School of Dancing	61
Victoria Park	22, 59
Warden Park Primary School	59, 72
Weald Theatre Group	61
Wesleyan Chapel	66
Wyatt, Revd Robert	30-31
Yapp, William	55

Notes

1. Twisleton.co.uk
2. *Haywards Heath in days gone by* Facebook group
3. John Twisleton, *Fifty Walks from Haywards Heath: A handbook for seeking space in Mid Sussex* (Amazon, 2020)
4. Wyn K Ford & AC Gabe, *The Metropolis of Mid Sussex - A history of Haywards Heath* (Charles Clarke, 1981) p1
5. *Metropolis of Mid Sussex* p65
6. *Fifty Walks from Haywards Heath* p58
7. *Metropolis of Mid Sussex* p3
8. Elizabeth Williamson, Tim Hudson, Jeremy Munson and Ian Nairn, *The Buildings of England - Sussex: West* (Yale University Press, 2019) p2
9. The first part of Chapter 3 is informed by a draft history of St Wilfrid's communicated to the author by former parish priest Fr Ray Smith 2019
10. *Metropolis of Mid Sussex* p36
11. John Twisleton, *Thirty Walks from Brighton Station: Catching sighs and sea air* (Amazon, 2020)
12. Text of Haywards Heath Council display board on Muster Green entitled 'English Civil War 1642-1646'
13. *Metropolis of Mid Sussex* p39-43
14. Communicated to the author by former parish priest Fr Ray Smith 2019
15. Margaret Nicolle, *William Allen, Quaker Friend of Lindfield 1770-1843* (Margaret Nicolle, 2001) p102
16. *William Allen - English Quaker* Wikipedia quote from self-sufficient settlement detailed in 'Colonies at Home'
17. *William Allen* p41

18	*William Allen* p57
19	*William Allen* p119-120
20	*William Allen* p134
21	Communicated to the author by Charles Tucker
22	*Mid Sussex Times* Tuesday 2 July 1912 ' Mr. Thomas Bannister, J.P. of Haywards Heath, dies at Seaford. Funeral at St Wilfrid's Church on Wednesday Afternoon'. Article in www.cuckfieldconnections.org.uk
23	Wilfrid Jackson, *Haywards Heath: A History & Celebration (*The Francis Frith Collection, 2005) p14
24	*On Call - St Francis Hospital* The Life and work of St Francis Hospital 1859-1995 (Mid Sussex NHS Trust, November 1995 Special Edition) p2
25	*On Call - St Francis Hospital* p2-3
26	*James Gardner,* Sweet Bells Jangled Out of Tune: A History of the Sussex Lunatic Asylum (St Francis Hospital) Haywards Heath (James Gardner, 1999) p284-285
27	*Haywards Heath: A History & Celebration* p39
28	*Metropolis of Mid Sussex* p159
29	Communicated to the author by Mike Lewis 2020
30	The middle of Chapter 9 is informed by the History section of Haywards Heath Town Football Club website https://hhtfc.co.uk/
31	*Metropolis of Mid Sussex* p112
32	Communicated to the author by Peter Miles
33	Communicated to the author by Charles Tucker
34	Albert H Gregory, *Mid-Sussex through the ages* (Charles Clarke (Haywards Heath) Ltd,1938) p11-12
35	*Metropolis of Mid Sussex* p189

Appendix 1

South Downs walks via Haywards Heath station

- ✔ View Sussex and the sea
- ✔ From the South Downs Way
- ✔ Gaining oxygen for the spirit
- ✔ On footpaths dry all year
- ✔ Leaving little carbon footprint

Choose from 20 walks, 3 miles to 19 miles long, leaving 7 Sussex stations speedily accessible from Haywards Heath and ending at 12 Sussex stations for your return.

Glynde to Lewes rail trail - 3 miles Turn left out of Glynde station and walk to the post office. Turn left then almost immediately right over the stile to ascend the path up Mount Caburn which runs with a fence to your left. At the gate go straight ahead with the tumulus on your left to the stile on the fence at the hill top. Continue down the other side following this path eventually skirting Lewes golf course to your right and then descend to Lewes station.

Southease to Glynde rail trail - 4 miles From Southease station follow the South Downs Way across the A26 Lewes to Newhaven road. Ascend the Downs enjoying panoramic views of Newhaven and Lewes. Before the transmitters turn left to follow the footpath down to the A27. Cross the road and walk on to Glynde station.

Falmer to Lewes rail trail - 5 miles From Falmer station adjacent to the football stadium head south via the university and up The Drove (B2123). After half a mile take the footpath on the left off the main road. After another half mile continue sharp right on the track as it crosses another one at a Newmarket Plantation. Continue on this track (Jugg's Road) with its scenic views as it descends via Kingston near Lewes into Southover and then proceed to Lewes station.

Falmer to Southease rail trail - 6 miles As in the previous walk from Falmer station head south via the university and up The Drove (B2123). After half a mile take the footpath on the left off the main road. After another half mile continue sharp right on the track as it crosses another one at a Newmarket Plantation. Continue on this track (Jugg's Road) but turn right above Kingston to continue along the South Downs Way enjoying views of Lewes and Rodmell to the beautiful Southease Church and then on to the station.

Hassocks to Falmer rail trail - 6 miles From Hassocks station follow the footpath besides the track heading towards Brighton. Cross the road junction after a mile and head across the sports field through Clayton up to Jack and Jill windmills. Head left and then take the right fork shortly after heading down via Lower Standean to Ditchling Road. Cross the road and turn right heading south on the footpath besides the road. After half a mile turn left and walk on to beautiful Stanmer village. Continue through the park and under the A27 to Falmer station.

Hassocks to Moulsecoomb rail trail - 6 miles As in the previous walk from Hassocks station follow the footpath besides the track heading towards Brighton. Cross the road junction after a mile and head across the sports field through Clayton up to Jack and Jill windmills. Head left and then take the right fork shortly after, heading down via Lower Standean to Ditchling Road. Cross the road and turn right heading south on the footpath through the woods besides the road. Cross the A27 at the junction with Ditchling Road heading down the road to Hollingbury for half a mile. Take the footpath on the left across open land with scenic views to Moulsecoomb station. Alternatively continue along the wooded footpath above the A27 to cross on the Coldean footbridge walking through the houses and open land to Moulsecoomb station.

Southease to Lewes rail trail - 7 miles From Southease station turn right to follow the South Downs Way across the A26 Lewes to Newhaven road. Ascend the Downs enjoying panoramic views of Newhaven and Lewes. Before the transmitters turn left to follow the footpath down to the A27. Cross the road and walk on past Glynde station to the post office. You can divert to see the Church and adjacent entrance to Glynde Place just up the road. Turn left via the post office then immediately right over the stile to ascend the path up Mount Caburn which runs with a fence to your left. At the gate go straight ahead with the tumulus on your left to the stile on the fence at the hilltop. Continue down the other side following this path skirting Lewes golf course to your right and descend to Lewes station.

Glynde to Berwick rail trail - 8 miles Turn right out of the station and walk down to the A27. Cross the main road and walk up the minor road ascending the Downs. Turn left at the top to pass the transmitters and continue descending before Alfriston to Berwick Church where you can view the wall paintings. Proceed from there north along the Vanguard Way to Berwick station.

Hassocks to Portslade rail trail - 8 miles From Hassocks station follow the footpath south beside the railway to the road and continue very carefully south along the road turning right at the riding school to head over the hills to Pyecombe. Cross the footbridge over the A23, ascend and then descend the path to Saddlescombe. Cross the road and continue on the path towards Devil's Dyke. Descend the footpath south towards Brighton & Hove from the road below the restaurant. Cross the A27 by footbridge either at Foredown Tower or above Hangleton and walk downhill to Portslade station.

Southease to Berwick rail trail - 8 miles As in the previous walk from Southease station turn right to follow the South Downs Way across the A26 Lewes to Newhaven road. Ascend the Downs enjoying panoramic views of Newhaven and Lewes continuing on the South Downs Way almost to Alfriston. Descend to Berwick Church where you can view the wall paintings. Proceed from there north along the Vanguard Way to Berwick station.

Berwick to Eastbourne rail trail - 9 miles Turn right out of the station and follow the road then footpath to the A27 and then the road to Alfriston. At the first junction turn left and after a quarter mile join the South Downs Way up Wilmington Hill, possibly diverting to see The Long Man of Wilmington. Descend to Jevington Church and ascend for the last stretch which crosses the golf course. Descend from the hills to Eastbourne station.

Hassocks to Lewes rail trail - 9 miles From Hassocks station follow the footpath besides the track heading towards Brighton. Cross the road junction after a mile and head across the sports field through Clayton up to Jack and Jill windmills. Head left and continue following the South Downs Way to Ditchling Beacon and on to Lewes enjoying views of Sussex and the sea. Return from Lewes station.

Southease to Brighton rail trail - 9 miles From Southease station turn left and walk past the Church up to the road. Turn right along the road and then left in a few hundred yards onto the South Downs Way. After half a mile continue straight ahead as the Way veers right and head for Telscombe village. Enjoy the panoramic view as you descend from there to Telscombe cliffs on the outskirts of Peacehaven. Cross the A259 and follow various cliff, road or under cliff walks through Saltdean and Rottingdean. After passing Brighton Marina and Pier turn inland again to reach Brighton station.

Hassocks to Fishersgate rail trail - 10 miles As in a previous walk from Hassocks station follow the footpath south to the road and continue very carefully south along the road turning right at the riding school to head over the hills to Pyecombe. Cross the footbridge over the A23, ascend and then descend the path to Saddlescombe. Cross the road and continue on the path towards Devil's Dyke. Descend from there on the South Downs Way continuing above Fulking to Truleigh Hill.

After the radio station turn left onto the lane which descends over Southwick Hill and down to Fishersgate station.

Seaford to Eastbourne rail trail - 10 miles From Seaford station head down Church Street towards the promenade. Turn left and continue up the cliffs along the Vanguard Way to Cuckmere Haven. At low tide you can wade across the river to start the Seven Sisters walk at Cliff End. At high tide the walk requires an additional 2 miles to follow the Cuckmere river upstream to the pub, cross the bridge and turn right to follow the downstream footpath which ascends to Cliff End. Follow the scenic Seven Sisters cliff walk via Birling Gap, Belle Tout disused Lighthouse and Beachy Head and descend to Eastbourne station.

Seaford to Berwick rail trail - 13 miles Turn right outside Seaford station. After half a mile turn left onto a footpath, continuing left again onto Alfriston Road. Follow the road over the Downs into historic Alfriston and then the Vanguard Way to Berwick station.

Southease to Eastbourne rail trail - 14 miles As in a previous walk from Southease station turn right to follow the South Downs Way across the A26 Lewes to Newhaven road. Ascend the Downs and continue on the Way enjoying panoramic views. Descend to Alfriston and then ascend the South Downs Way again up Wilmington Hill, possibly diverting to see The Long Man of Wilmington. Descend to Jevington Church and ascend for the last stretch which crosses the golf course. Descend from the hills to Eastbourne station.

Hassocks to Plumpton rail trail - 15 miles From Hassocks station follow the footpath besides the track heading towards Brighton. Cross the road junction after a mile and head across the sports field through Clayton up to Jack and Jill windmills. Head left and continue on the South Downs Way. A mile or so after Ditchling Beacon head downhill on one of the paths towards Plumpton College crossing the main road. Continue in the same northerly direction either on the footpath east of the College or Plumpton Lane further east. The walk concludes by following the perimeter of the Race Course to Plumpton station.

Lewes to Eastbourne rail trail - 16 miles Turn right out of Lewes station, right and then right again over the river along Cliffe High Street and then up Chapel Hill. Follow the footpath skirting the golf course towards Mount Caburn descending on the footpath to Glynde. Head south through the village, cross the A27 and walk up the minor road ascending the Downs. Turn left at the top to pass the transmitters and continue on the South Downs Way to Eastbourne and the station.

Hassocks to Worthing rail trail - 19 miles As in a previous walk from Hassocks station follow the footpath south to the road and continue very carefully south along the road turning right at the riding school to head over the hills to Pyecombe. Cross the footbridge over the A23, ascend and then descend the path to Saddlescombe. Cross the road and continue on the path towards Devil's Dyke. Descend from there on the South Downs Way continuing above Fulking to Truleigh Hill. Continue past the Youth Hostel down to the A283. Continue on the Way across the road and the River Adur to walk south of Steyning, possibly diverting to see the historic St. Botolph's Church. Head up Annington Hill over Lancing College and continue on the South Downs Way until it reaches the road. Go left and descend Titch Hill turning right a mile down at the farm. Follow the footpath to descend Lambleys Lane down to the A27. Cut through the housing estates to Broadwater Road and down to Worthing station.

Appendix 2

London sights via Haywards Heath station

- ✔ Twenty London sights
- ✔ Free to view
- ✔ On foot from a rail or underground station
- ✔ Leaving little carbon footprint

Big Ben clock tower stands 316 feet (96 metres) over Parliament, affectionately called after the nickname for the largest of its five bells. Catch a train to Victoria Station and walk down Victoria Street to Parliament Square where you can also see statues of Winston Churchill and Nelson Mandela.

Borough Market grew up on the south bank of the earliest bridge across the Thames and traces back to 1014. It is adjacent to Southwark Cathedral which can be visited without charge. Catch a train to London Bridge Station where the Market and Cathedral are well signed.

British Museum in Bloomsbury founded in 1753 charts the story of human culture from its beginnings to the present. The Museum's collection of 140 mummies and coffins is the largest outside Cairo. Catch a train to London Victoria and take a 38 bus or a tube to Holborn where the Museum is well signed.

Buckingham Palace Changing the Guard takes place every Monday, Wednesday, Friday and Sunday lasting from 1045am -

1130am. Catch a train to London Victoria, walk left at the front of the station then turn right onto Buckingham Palace Road and head along to the pedestrianised area in front of the Palace.

Covent Garden is an open area between the West End and the City of London east of Trafalgar Square formerly a fruit, vegetable and flower market and now a weatherproof tourist attraction with free live entertainment. Catch a train to London Victoria and take a 24, 26 or 38 bus or a tube to Covent Garden.

Greenwich on the Thames is famous for its world dividing Meridian line and Observatory, the Cutty Sark, National Maritime Museum, Old Royal Naval College and Queen's House. Catch a train to London Bridge and take a 188 bus or follow signs to the pier and catch a river boat to Greenwich.

Horse Guards Two splendidly clothed sentries on horseback are on duty 10am - 4pm in Whitehall at the entrance to Horse Guards Parade, a large space used for parades also accessible from St James' Park. Catch a train to London Victoria and take a 24 or 26 bus to Whitehall.

Hyde Park contains the large Serpentine and Long Water lakes. Speakers' Corner at its top right hand corner is famous for lively Sunday debates. Catch a train to London Victoria and head left from the station forecourt walking along Grosvenor Gardens and Grosvenor Place up to Hyde Park's south east entrance.

Imperial War Museum founded 1917 is one of five national museums serving the study and understanding of the history of modern war and 'wartime experience'. Artefacts range from naval guns to drones. Catch a train to London Victoria and take a number 3 Crystal Palace bus.

Kensington hosts the Natural History, Science and Victoria & Albert Museums as well as Albert Memorial, Brompton Oratory, Kensington Palace and the Royal Albert Hall. Catch a train to London Victoria and take a 52 Willesden bus or tube to South Kensington where these sights are signed.

London Eye diagonally across the Thames from Big Ben is a grand sight and in 2024 the nation's most popular paid tourist attraction. The Wheel is 135 metres (443 ft) tall and 120 metres (394 ft) diameter. Catch a train to London Victoria and walk along Victoria Street or take bus/tube to Westminster station.

Piccadilly Circus though on a major traffic junction is famed as a pedestrian meeting place at the Shaftesbury Memorial Fountain. The Circus is famous for its video display and neon signs mounted on adjacent buildings. Catch a train to London Victoria and take the 38 bus or tube to Piccadilly Circus.

Sky Garden is a garden with scenic views opened 2015 up a skyscraper nicknamed 'The Walkie-Talkie'. Access is free but online booking is essential. Catch a train to London Bridge then walk across the Bridge, right along East Cheap then left along Philpot Lane or take a 17, 149 or 344 bus.

St Paul's Cathedral has free access to daily worship eg 5pm weekday Sung Evensong. Worship has been offered on the site since 604. Christopher Wren rebuilt St Paul's after the 1666 fire of London. It was London's tallest building until 1963. Catch a train to City Thameslink and walk up Ludgate Hill.

Tower of London is a riverside stone fortress adjacent to Tower Bridge built by William the Conqueror starting in 1078. It was a prison and place of execution and the Crown Jewels are kept there. Catch a train to London Bridge, walk across Tooley Street and head right for Tower Bridge.

Trafalgar Square was established near the historic Charing Cross to commemorate the Battle of Trafalgar (1805). Besides Nelson's Column, sights include the National Gallery, National Portrait Gallery and St Martin's Church. Catch a train to London Bridge then another train to Charing Cross station.

Wallace Collection displaying about 5,500 works of art was given to the nation by Lady Wallace in 1897. The collection in Hertford House behind Selfridges can be viewed free of charge. Catch a train to London Victoria then 390 bus or tube to Bond Street, cross Oxford Street and go along Duke Street.

Wellcome Collection Henry Wellcome (1853-1936) amassed a collection of books, paintings and objects linked to medicine's development across the world. The museum and library founded 2007 provides access to this collection. Catch a train to St Pancras, head down to Euston Road and walk to the right.

Westminster Abbey is a church historically linked to the royal family complementing London's Cathedral of St Paul. It contains St Edward's shrine and is used for coronations. There is free access to 5pm weekday Sung Evensong. Catch a train to London Victoria and walk to the Abbey along Victoria Street.

Westminster Cathedral is the Mother Church for Roman Catholics in England and Wales. Designed in Byzantine style by John Francis Bentley, the brick Cathedral, opened 1903, has a prayerful atmosphere and free entry. Catch a train to London Victoria and the Cathedral is adjacent to the station.

JOHN TWISLETON

Appendix 3

History of Presentation Church

Abridged version of the talk given by Fr John Twisleton to Women's Fellowship 4 July 2024 at Centenary Hall

William Allen's benevolence in founding the 'America colony' was succeeded by that of Mary Otter in founding Presentation Church off New England Road RH16 3LE. Granddaughter of the Bishop of Chichester William Otter she became 'District Visitor' for the colony arranging talks in one of the thatched cottages from Lent 1880 paving the way for a mission church served by St Wilfrid's first assistant curate, The Revd Thomas Wyatt son of the first Vicar. The iron building was enlarged in 1886 and dedicated to recall the Presentation of the Infant Christ in the Temple. Within a decade plans were made and executed to provide a more permanent brick church building which started services in 1897. By then Fr Thomas had succeeded his father as Vicar of St Wilfrid's Parish.

The services at first were a weekly Sunday afternoon service of Evensong and an early Holy Communion service on the fourth Sunday of the month. In 1921 Miss Otter paid for the font which was dedicated that year. Mary Otter died on 27th December 1925 and was interred at Cowfold Parish Church where her father had been Vicar. Fr Thomas Wyatt's grave is prominent in Western Road cemetery as his father Fr Robert Wyatt's is prominent in St Wilfrid's Churchyard representing their missionary work up and down the hill.

Presentation Church member Tony Heald recalls: 'I was born in Western Road and baptised in Presentation Church 1936. I started Sunday School at four years old as my mother was a regular church goer. I started primary school in the old St.Wilfrids where Zizzi's restaurant is now situated. I enjoyed going to school although the teachers were quite strict. If you misbehaved you got the cane across your knuckles! I joined the church choir when I was seven continuing until my voice broke, and then I pumped the organ for a while which at that time was up by the lectern. Eventually the organ was taken away and electrified and re-installed in its present position. At age sixteen Dennis Howard and I started a Subbuteo table football club for boys in the church hall. We were advised by his dad and used to play Saturday evenings. This continued until the fire that burnt the hall down. When I was about eleven I was confirmed at St. Wilfrid's church and became an altar server. I also started helping with the Sunday School around this time. When Brenda and I started going out together we both enjoyed going to the square dance club that met in the hall, a hobby we enjoyed for several years. My mum ran the Women's Fellowship for many years, well into her eighties'.

Tony's wife Brenda Heald recalls: 'I remember the Church of the Presentation from a very young age as my mother was a regular attendee. The Sunday School was in the old corrugated tin hut in front of the church and was run by a lovely old lady with the sweetest smile and twinkly eyes – Miss Roser. She left a lasting memory of kindness I'm sure she was unaware of. I was confirmed at about twelve, which made a big impression on me'.

Presentation Church member Michael Loosen joined Presentation choir in 1962 and writes: 'A youth club was held in the hall every Friday evening. After choir practice several of us popped into the hall to listen to the latest hit tunes of the day by artists such as Cliff Richard, Del Shannon and Bobby Lee. It was a very good scene for the local kids of the early 60s'.

When Presentation Church was built a new house was also built, 87 New England Road known as 'Woodside' accessed via the narrow roadway alongside the church. This was purchased by the parish in 1959 for the Priest in Charge of the Presentation. The purchase gave the parish a firm legacy for the future realised 1993-5 in the building of Marylands and a new Vicarage in the land previously serving as the old Vicarage garden.

Presentation Church member Janie Bishop writes of the old Vicarage garden: 'When we came to live in Bentswood Road in April 1961 it consisted of a large lawn between the Vicarage house and ours, and an orchard of apple, pear and plum trees covering the whole of what is now Marylands, complete with an enormous Nissen hut for keeping hens, and a disused pigsty down in the furthest corner. On the other side of the vicarage (where the church car park is now) was a pond with bull-rushes I understood it to be fed by the rainwater drains of New England Road, and our neighbour stopped us making a compost heap at the top of our garden, explaining that we had to keep the ditch clear so that any overflow from the pond could drain away. The boundary between our garden and the vicarage lawn was marked by a tall hedge of mature mixed native trees: holly, hawthorn, and hazel, with one or two sycamores, a splendid row of beech on the north boundary and an oak tree behind the pond (felled in 2023). I remember the arrival in 1962 of the Reverend Tony Oliver, his wife Audrey and their two grown-up sons. I understood that there had been another son, killed as a schoolboy when he picked up an unexploded grenade on a South Coast beach near his boarding school. One of the sons was profoundly deaf, but Mrs Oliver had taught him to speak and to lip-read. Tony Oliver was a retired naval officer, and Audrey an archetypal officer's wife, with endearing eccentricities. For instance, she would take her mending basket, and her old dog, to committee meetings, where the prayers at the beginning might be enlivened by the dog's claws rattling over the lino, or even better, by an errant cotton-reel rolling across the floor. They loved the garden and used every inch of it, holding garden parties and fetes on the lawn, as well as Guide, Brownie, Scout and Cub meetings there or in the orchard. They made a vegetable patch, and even experimented with making wine from the grapevine in the conservatory and cider from the fruits of the orchard. The cellar came into its own for this enterprise. Their other son caused a sensation by opening Haywards Heath's first launderette in Sussex Road, next door to the Baptist Church (then Primitive Methodist) where the kebab shop is now. It was called "Revilo" (Oliver spelt backwards) and I still have the script of a sketch performed by the St Wilfrid's Fellowship Fishers youth club, poking fun at this innovation and using every cliché and in-joke imaginable'.

When Anne and I arrived in 2017 at 13 Marylands our house deeds indicated the land title transferred to its first occupants 5 October 1994 after the house was completed. The old parish curate's house on William Allen Lane had been sold in 1997 to provide some of the finance for the new Presentation Vicarage. The church was also refitted, repainted and rewired under the careful management of non stipendiary curate The Revd Douglas Hollis who retired in 1997.

In the last sixty years Presentation Church has been overseen by five Rectors: Roy Hicks (1962-1977), John Bernardi (1977-1987), Ian Brackley (1988-1996), Ray Smith (1996-2020) and Edward Pritchett (2021-). Under their oversight Team Vicars or Assistant Curates resident in Presentation Vicarage have been: John Rowlands (1958-1962), Tony Oliver (1962-1968), David James (1968-1971), Kenneth Bradshaw (1971-1982), Keith Swaby (1982-1995), Derek Coombes (1997-2007) and Alison Letschka (2008-2012) with self supporting clergy the late Douglas Hollis, Jean Sedgley, David Young and currently Mike Clark, Deacon Carolyn Scott and John Twisleton. As Chichester Diocesan Mission & Renewal Adviser 2001-2009 and then Rector of St Giles, Horsted Keynes 2009-2017 I have been involved in the mission and ministry of both the Presentation and St Wilfrid's now from my chosen base in another former daughter Church, The Society parish of St Richard.

Like many churches, since 2012 without a resident priest, Presentation Church relies more on her lay leaders to keep its sense of purpose and belonging. Presentation Church with its warm liturgical tradition is blessed by its local following evident on Sunday, at the Monday lunch club and other hall activities. The church has an evident outreach to Bentswood through a generous membership operating under Christ's command: 'Give and it will be given to you' (Luke 6:38).

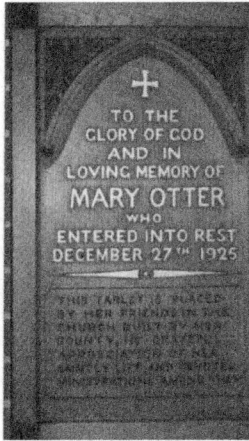

Photograph and plaque honouring Mary Otter in Presentation Church

Presentation Church with the original Hall destroyed by fire in 1978 rebuilt 1983

About the author

John Twisleton has lived in Haywards Heath or its surrounds for 23 years working as a diocesan mission enabler across Sussex 2001-2009, Rector of St Giles, Horsted Keynes 2009-2017 and assistant priest serving St Richard, Haywards Heath, St Mary, Balcombe, St John the Evangelist, Burgess Hill, St Bartholomew, Brighton and Ardingly College within the Anglican Church since retiring as a parish priest in 2017.

An ideas and people person, poet, priest, writer and broadcaster, John has a heart for the well being of Haywards Heath which includes building a better grasp of local history. With a background in polymer research and previous church postings in Coventry, Guyana, London and his native Yorkshire, Fr John is passionate about writing, spirituality, and using his skills to serve the community not least as a digital access enabler. He serves as a spiritual director with the London Centre for Spiritual Direction accessible www.lcsd.org.uk. helping people online or face to face to find the best way ahead through discerning God's movement in their lives.

John has been married to Anne since 1988 and has three sons located in London, Burgess Hill, and Brighton. He is a member of the northern branch of the ancient Twisleton family with connection to the southern Twisleton-Wykeham-Fiennes branch. He serves as a dedicated carer for his wife who was diagnosed with Alzheimer's in 2022. His personal website contains his poems, articles and broadcasts and summaries of his twenty published books: **Twisleton.co.uk**. The six books summarised below might be of interest to readers of this book.

Fifty Walks from Haywards Heath

Sub-titled 'A handbook for seeking space in Mid Sussex' this book celebrates the riches of a town at the heart of Sussex. Through detailed walk routes with schematic illustrations by Rebecca Twisleton, formerly Padgham, John Twisleton outlines routes from one to thirteen miles with an eye to local history and replenishment of the spirit.

Forty Walks from Ally Pally

John Twisleton explores the byways of Barnet, Camden, Enfield and Haringey with an eye to green spaces, local history and a replenishment of the spirit. The routes, which vary in length between one mile and twenty miles, exploit the public transport network, and are well designed for family outings. The author provides here a practical handbook for seeking space in North London.

Thirty walks from Brighton Station

A practical handbook for exploring the city and its surrounds reaching beyond the daytripper's duo of Pier and Pavilion to two hundred and sixty six sights with commentary on many of these. John Twisleton describes his motivation being linked, as a historian, to love for Brighton & Hove, as a walker, to the replenishment of body, mind and spirit attained in that pursuit and as an environmentalist to serving recreation with low carbon footprint. Illustrations: Rebecca Twisleton formerly Padgham

A History of St Giles Church, Horsted Keynes

Besides being the burial place of former UK Prime Minister Harold Macmillan (1894-1986) and mystic ecumenist Archbishop Robert Leighton (1611-1684) St Giles, Horsted Keynes has association with the history of Sussex back to the 8th century. As 53rd Rector (2009-2017) John Twisleton wrote this illustrated history with the assistance of church members.

Elucidations - Light on Christian controversies

As an Anglocatholic priest who experienced a faith crisis enlarging God for him, John Twisleton, former scientist, sheds light on thoughtful allegiance to Christianity in the 21st century condensing down thinking on controversial topics ranging from self-love to unanswered prayer, Mary to antisemitism, suffering to same sex unions, charismatic experience to the ordination of women, hell to ecology and trusting the Church, a total of twenty five essays.

Journeying Together

In 1988 John and Anne Twisleton were married in Guyana where they helped train indigenous priests returning to the UK and service in Coventry, London and Sussex. 'Journeying Together' is a double autobiography illustrated by Anne's paintings. It celebrates with John another marriage, that of science and Christianity, and his exercise of the priesthood. In Anne's story we present the benefits of social engagement tackling illiteracy and poverty. The last chapters touch on living with Alzheimer's disease, Anne's experience and John's as her carer, completing a book provoking thought and warming the heart.

Haywards Heath

At the heart of Sussex
surrounded by green land,
an inviting place to be:
Haywards Heath.

An historic junction
with commanding heights
where Roman roads
cross the High Weald.

London's love for Brighton
put our town on the map
when their rail link
got forced our way.

A commuter town
with outgoing workers
yet a sight seeing hub
with incoming folk.

Two centuries of life
celebrating health care
and farming through to
enterprise galore.

Haywards Heath
at the heart of Sussex
has a heart of its own
and abundant spirit.

John Twisleton 16 July 2024

Printed in Great Britain
by Amazon